Library Technology
REPORTS

Expert Guides to Library Systems and Services

Consolidation of the Library Technology Industry

Marshall Breeding

ALA TechSource
alatechsource.org

American Library Association

Library Technology
REPORTS

ALA TechSource purchases fund advocacy, awareness, and accreditation programs for library professionals worldwide.

Volume 56, Number 8
Consolidation of the Library Technology Industry
ISBN: 978-0-8389-4679-4
DOI: https://doi.org/10.5860/ltr.56n8

American Library Association
225 N. Michigan Ave., Suite 1300
Chicago, IL 60601-7616 USA
alatechsource.org
800-545-2433, ext. 4299
312-944-6780
312-280-5275 (fax)

Advertising Representative
Patrick Hogan
phogan@ala.org
312-280-3240

Editor
Patrick Hogan
phogan@ala.org
312-280-3240

Copy Editor
Judith Lauber

Production
ALA Production Services

Cover Design
Alejandra Diaz and ALA Production Services

Library Technology Reports (ISSN 0024-2586) is published eight times a year (January, March, April, June, July, September, October, and December) by American Library Association, 225 N. Michigan Ave., Suite 1300, Chicago, IL 60601-7616. It is managed by ALA TechSource, a unit of the publishing department of ALA. Periodical postage paid at Chicago, Illinois, and at additional mailing offices. POSTMASTER: Send address changes to Library Technology Reports, 225 N. Michigan Ave., Suite 1300, Chicago, IL 60601-7616.

ALA TechSource
alatechsource.org

About the Author

Marshall Breeding is an independent consultant, speaker, and author. He is the creator and editor of the Library Technology Guides website, editor of *Smart Libraries Newsletter*, and a columnist for *Computers in Libraries*. He has authored the annual "Automation Marketplace" feature published most recently in *American Libraries*. He has also edited or authored several books, including *Cloud Computing for Libraries*. Formerly the director for innovative technology and research for the Vanderbilt University Library, he regularly teaches workshops and gives presentations internationally at library conferences.

Abstract

This issue of *Library Technology Reports* offers an in-depth analysis of the vendor and product environment in libraries over the past thirty years. Mergers and acquisitions have accelerated in the past decade, yet the pattern of maintaining products has nevertheless presented libraries with options and a competitive environment. The report draws extensively from data on vendors and product implementations.

Subscriptions

alatechsource.org/subscribe

Contents

Chapter 1

Introduction to the 2020 Library Technology Industry

Libraries depend on a set of commercial providers to develop and support their core technology products. No library has the resources to, nor the interest in, creating its own software. The work and activities conducted by a library are varied and complex and require the support of sophisticated technology systems. The differing needs of each type of library further add to the complexity of software development. Libraries require specialized technology products created by organizations with a deep understanding of their operational workflows and the services offered to their users.

Given their reliance on acquiring their main technology products from a commercial market, libraries expect a competitive business environment. A healthy industry would offer multiple viable products that vie for selection based on functional capabilities, vendor performance, and price.

The organizations that comprise the library technology industry include a diverse array. The industry includes both for-profit and nonprofit corporations that vary in size from small companies to very large-scale businesses with earnings in the billion-dollar range. Ownership arrangements include companies owned and managed by their founders and others controlled through some type of investment firm.

The vendors offering technology products to libraries face a difficult business environment. Even though the number of libraries may seem vast, the quantity of potential opportunities is limited and even further constrained by libraries' modest budgets and allocations for technology products and services. The library market is not monolithic. Rather it is segmented by size and type. Public, academic, school, and special libraries have increasingly diverged in the ways they serve their constituent communities and accordingly gravitate toward different technology products. Small libraries may not be well served by the complex systems that large institutions require. A limited overall market requiring specialized products for each subsector presents steep challenges to companies looking for sustainable business opportunities.

The consolidation of the industry through mergers and acquisitions of companies and products stands out as the prevailing theme over the last decade or two. Competitors have converged; some have been absorbed into top-level companies with business interests beyond the technology sector.

Libraries have a great deal at stake in the nature of the technology industry upon which they depend for products and services essential to their organizations. They will be greatly hindered in their missions should there not be adequate technology systems to support their operations and service delivery. Libraries would not be well served by an industry that fails to offer effective products or where the costs of desired products exceed budget realities.

This report takes a close look at the dynamics of the library technology industry and assesses the impact consolidation has made on the products and services available. Aggressive consolidation raises some important questions: Has the number of companies been reduced to the point where competition is not able to moderate pricing? Is the industry able to produce products and services to meet the needs of libraries? Will this trend toward consolidation result in monopolies in each subsector?

The following chapter examines the current state of the library industry. It provides an overview of the organizations involved and documents some of the patterns of consolidation seen over their business histories. Chapter 3 presents a study of the historical competitive trends in play since 1990 based on a new analysis of data representing the products installed in libraries each year during this period. The final chapter brings together some of the observations and suggests some of the possibilities that may be in store for the industry in future years.

This report builds on prior work of the author. He has chronicled the library technology industry as the editor and primary contributor of *Smart Libraries Newsletter*, published by ALA TechSource. The articles in the newsletter provide extensive details and context about major industry events as they transpire. Likewise, the "Library Systems Report" published annually in *American Libraries* helps document the evolution of the industry, including detailed data provided by the vendors represented. Library Technology Guides, especially the libraries.org directory, represents a unique data set of the sequence of automation systems used by libraries, which provides a quantitative measure of industry trends.

Library Technology Guides
https://librarytechnology.org

Chapter 2

Industry Dynamics and Trends

The library technology industry is a complex set of organizations with the common characteristic of offering technology products and services to libraries. This group includes an interesting mix of organizations, ranging from large multinational businesses to small companies offering more specialized products, and includes some nonprofit organizations. The many organizations represented and their associated business dynamics cannot be boiled down into a few simplistic trends. Rather, there are many layers, subsectors, and special circumstances that coexist within the broad trends that dominate news headlines. Industry consolidation stands out as the key trend. But it is also important to see consolidation in the context of other threads of activity.

Bringing Together a Fragmented Industry

Prior to the last decade, the library technology industry would be considered a fragmented business environment. Many small and midsize companies, each with limited capacities for product development, competed within a limited market. This period was characterized by a large selection of products, but with little differentiation in functional capabilities. The functional model of the integrated library system was well established, with specific expectations for each module. To maintain a position in the market, each ILS product had to meet a detailed checklist of requirements that were specified in detail in procurement documents. The rise and fall of ILS products were largely driven by cycles in technology. Products created for mainframes were replaced by others following a client/server architecture, which in turn were replaced by or evolved into web-based systems. Products built for operating environments that became obsolete, such as VAX/VMS or Pick, eventually gave way to those based on Unix or Windows.

The integrated library system was the mainstay of the library technology industry through about 2010. The business overhead involved with multiple companies producing very similar products proved difficult to sustain. Mergers or acquisitions among direct competitors narrowed the number of companies in the industry. The number of products available was reduced at a much slower pace. While business advantages were gained by combining companies, maintaining products was essential to minimize disruption to the libraries involved and to retain the customers of the acquired entity.

During this phase of the industry, many commercial and library-based projects offered ILS products offering similar functionality. Some of these products were

- Dynix Systems
- OCLC Local Systems Division: LS/2000
- Data Phase ALIS I
- Avitar
- NOTIS
- Sirsi Corporation Unicorn
- INNOPAC/Millennium/Sierra: Innovative Interfaces
- Gaylord: Galaxy, Polaris
- Atlas: Data Research Associates
- MultiLIS:
- INLEX
- Data Trek
- EOS International
- TINLIB IME Systems
- CARL
- The Library Corporation: BiblioFile, Library. Solution
- BASIS plus: Information Dimensions
- Aleph: Ex Libris
- Voyager: Endeavor Information Systems
- Horizon: Dynix
- VTLS Virtua
- Winnebago Spectrum
- Athena: Nichols Advanced Technology
- InfoCentre: Sagebrush Corporation

International products included

- Bibliotheca BOND
- HKA BicatWise
- Amlib
- OLIB
- Sunrise: Sisis

During this phase of the industry, the companies developing and supporting each of these ILS products were generally smaller than the consolidated companies active today. The development capacity of a vendor can be measured by the number of personnel allocated to product development. The vendor survey for the "Library Systems Report" requests this data. Not all vendors supply these statistics, and data is not available prior to 2002. The available data for 2005 provides a glimpse of the size of some of the companies active at that time and their relative capacity for product development. Some of these companies no longer exist as separate entities because they were absorbed through corporate mergers.

Table 2.1 shows a selection of the personnel statistics from some of the larger companies active in 2005. SirsiDynix, immediately following the merger of Sirsi Corporation and Dynix, ranked as the largest, with 679 total personnel. As the two antecedent companies integrated, the company slimmed down to 380 in 2011, with 84 dedicated to development. Overall, the largest of these companies would be considered midsize in today's environment.

For comparison, table 2.2 presents the 2019 personnel statistics for a selection of companies. These statistics reveal the scale of the larger organizations and their relative development capacity. Between 2005 and 2019, Ex Libris expanded its overall personnel to 980 and its development group to 283. While sheer numbers do not guarantee quality or quantity of product development, these numbers are consistent with the ambitious development agenda that has produced some of the major products implemented in the academic library sector.

It is also interesting to note some of the statistics for companies that have not been involved in mergers and acquisitions. The Library Corporation was at its peak in 2005 with a total of 210 personnel employed; that number has since diminished to 117, with 45 devoted to development. Auto-Graphics has contracted somewhat from the 32 employed in 2005 to 28 today, with 5 devoted to product development. Book Systems has expanded a bit from 53 in 2005 to 68 today.

These personnel statistics over time suggest that outside of involvement with mergers, companies may struggle to hold their ground. Even if they maintain their size and capacity, they are increasingly dwarfed as new powerhouse companies are assembled. The demands of product development through new generations of technology and in response to changing realities of libraries may exceed the modest capabilities of small and midsize companies. Some may be able to hold on to niche markets, but there are no examples of small companies entering the market and gaining a dominant position in the absence of business acquisitions.

The Pervasive Pattern of Consolidation

Throughout the recent history of the library technology industry, there has been a continual series of business transactions. While some were simple changes in ownership, most resulted in the contraction of the number of vendors in the field through business acquisitions. Though some of these events were positioned as mergers among equals, there are no examples in the library technology industry where both

Table 2.1
2005 vendor personnel statistics

Company	Year	Development	Support	Sales	Admin	Other	Total
Endeavor Information Systems	2005	49	65	25	12	5	156
SirsiDynix	2005	153	391	77	55	3	679
Innovative Interfaces, Inc.	2005	66	171	32	26		295
Ex Libris	2005	57	93	39	23	49	261
EOS International	2005	24	26	24	4	1	79
Follett	2005	45	72	72	9	47	245
The Library Corporation	2005	70	85	22	12	21	210
Auto-Graphics, Inc.	2005	7	9	8	4	4	32
Book Systems	2005	12	18	17	4	2	53

Table 2.2
2019 vendor personnel statistics

Company	Year	Development	Support	Sales	Admin	Other	Total
Follett	2019	156	199	335	14	1,054	1,758
Ex Libris	2019	283	464	153	80		980
SirsiDynix	2019	127	150	50	34	26	387
The Library Corporation	2019	45	35	14	6	17	117
Auto-Graphics, Inc.	2019	5	9	5	1	8	28
Book Systems	2019	22	24	16	4	2	68

incumbent owners retained a long-term ownership stake in the combined organization.

These rounds of acquisitions resulted in a concentration of strategic library technology products within the portfolios of a small set of large-scale companies. ProQuest, Follett, and EBSCO Information Services have acquired or created core technology products as part of their broader offerings of products and services for libraries and related organizations. Each of these companies has annual revenues approaching or beyond a billion dollars.

A set of organizational charts provide a pictorial history of the development of these companies (figures 2.1–2.5, 2.8). These visualizations were developed by the author, published on Library Technology Guides, and are updated as additional events transpire. Detailed accounts of major events since about 2005 have been documented in *Smart Libraries Newsletter* and the annual "Library Systems Report."

ProQuest

ProQuest has emerged as the largest provider of technology products and services for academic and research libraries, which complements the database and other content products that were its traditional mainstay.

The ownership arrangements for ProQuest are complex. ProQuest is part of Cambridge Information Group, which is owned by the family of Robert N. Snyder. In addition to CIG, ProQuest has minority ownership by other major investors. From 2007 through 2013, ABRY Partners was a major investor. Goldman Sachs acquired the share held by ABRY in 2013. In 2019, Atairos made a major investment in ProQuest, gaining the largest minority stake in the company after CIG. At that time Goldman Sachs drew down its investment, though it retained a residual stake in the company.

Multiple threads of business activities transpired to shape ProQuest in its current form as one of the largest companies serving libraries. ProQuest has a lengthy corporate history, tracing its roots to University Microfilms International, established in 1938 by Eugene B. Power. The company became a major competitor in the library content sphere through multiple business events, including its acquisition by Bell and Howell and subsequent acquisition of other information companies such as Chadwyck-Healy, Micromedia, and SIRS Publishing. The company came more into its current form in 2007 when it was acquired by Cambridge Information Group, which at that time included Cambridge Scientific Abstracts and Bowker. Subsequent content acquisitions included Dialog (2008), Ebrary (2011), Electronic Book Library (2013), and Alexander Street (2016).

ProQuest expanded into the library technology sector through another set of events. This chain of activity began with its acquisition in 2004 of Serials Solutions, a rising star in the electronic resource management sector that was founded in 2000 with a set of products based on a well-regarded knowledge base of e-journal holdings. Under the leadership of Jane Burke, with previous executive roles for CLSI, Endeavor Information Systems and NOTIS Systems, Serials Solutions produced a successful line of workflow products for electronic resource management, and in 2009 it launched Summon as the first index-based discovery service able to address article-level content spanning almost all scholarly resources. Serials Solutions eventually morphed into the Workflow Solutions division of ProQuest. Other technology and workflow products acquired included AquaBrower Library in 2007 and WebFeat federated search solution in 2008.

For information on ProQuest's expansion, see

Marshall Breeding, "ProQuest Unifies Its Business, Drops Serials Solutions Brand," *Smart Libraries Newsletter,* March 2014, https://librarytechnology.org/document/19031.

In 2011, ProQuest, via its Serials Solutions division, launched a development initiative to create a library services platform, initially named its Web-Scale Management Solution and later branded as Intota. This project saw progress, though not on pace with Ex Libris Alma and OCLC WorldShare Management Services. Intota Assessment, the initial module of the platform, was released in 2013 with the involvement of a group of development partner libraries. Development of the full Intota platform continued through 2015, when ProQuest acquired Ex Libris. At that time further development of Intota halted, though libraries that had implemented Intota Assessment or other components of the platform continued to receive support.

The acquisition of Ex Libris by ProQuest propelled the company into the leading position as a technology provider to academic and research libraries. Ex Libris had consistently grown through an ambitious product development agenda and business acquisitions supported through multiple rounds of private equity investment. Emerging as a technology spin-off of Hebrew University of Jerusalem, Ex Libris saw considerable success marketing its Aleph ILS to libraries in multiple global regions. Ex Libris acquired the German DABIS system in 1997. Ex Libris increased its market share substantially in 2006 through the acquisition of the Voyager ILS from Elsevier. Its 2019 acquisition of RapidILL from Colorado State University strengthened its position in the resource sharing sector.

Ex Libris has seen multiple rounds of ownership and investment. Following its initial ownership by its founding university and a set of venture capital investors, the company has seen four successive acquisition transactions: Francisco Partners (June 2006), Leeds Equity (2008), Golden Gate Capital (2012), and ProQuest (2015). Through each of these investments the company substantially increased its valuation and created or acquired new products. Private equity investors usually hold their portfolio companies for a limited time. When large companies such as ProQuest make strategic acquisitions, those acquired companies become permanent extensions of their organization. Ex Libris has become well integrated into ProQuest. Matti Shem Tov, the former CEO of Ex Libris, became president and CEO of ProQuest in mid-2017, and Oren Beit-Arie, chief strategy officer of Ex Libris, was named to a similar position for ProQuest in June 2018.

Following the investment of Atairos in July 2019, ProQuest further expanded its involvement in the library technology arena with the acquisition of Innovative Interfaces in a transaction that closed in January 2020. Innovative had previously acquired Polaris

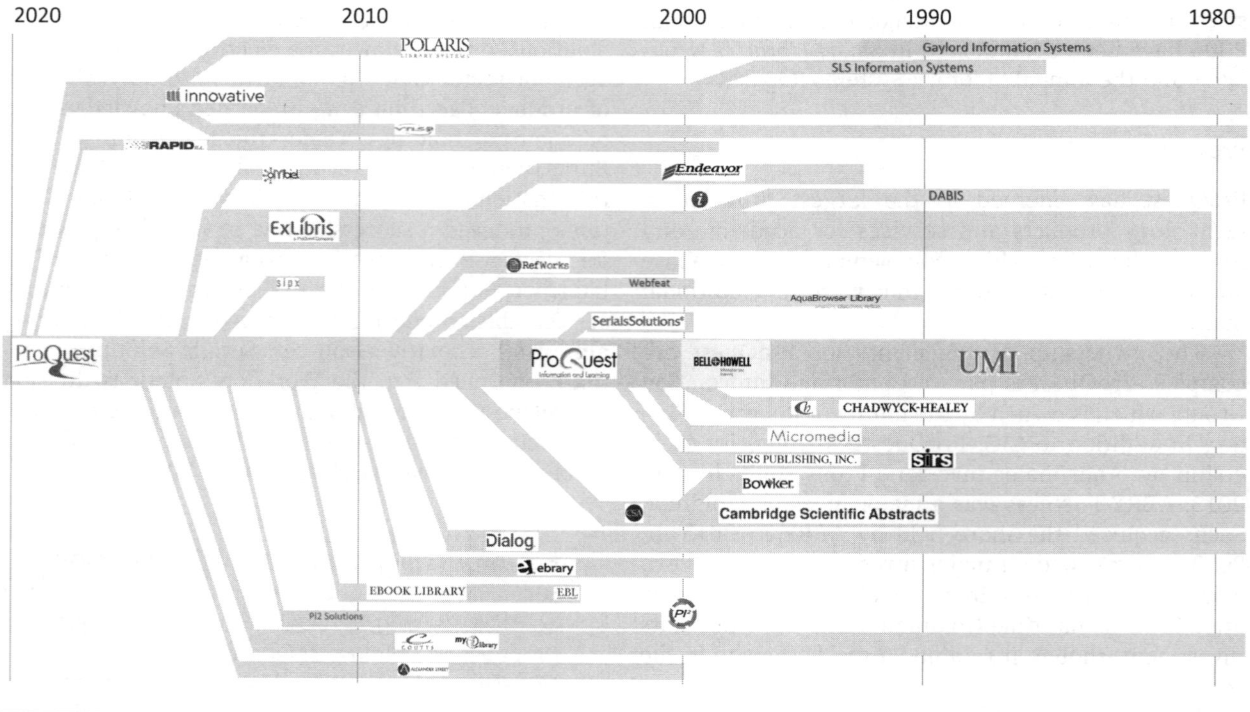

Figure 2.1
Development of ProQuest

(April 2014) and VTLS (June 2014). The acquisition of Innovative incrementally expanded ProQuest's position in the academic library sector and represented its initial entry into the public library technology sector. The acquisition of Innovative by ProQuest is currently under review by the US Federal Trade Commission. Business and product integration processes have been paused until completion of the review. Figure 2.1 illustrates ProQuest's development over time.

EBSCO Information Services

EBSCO Information Services, with annual revenue exceeding $2 billion,[1] ranks as a much larger company than ProQuest, though it has had less involvement with the library technology industry. The company has primarily based its business on subject databases and other content products and emerged as the leading provider of services for managing library journal subscriptions. With the acquisition of YBP Library Services, EBSCO also offers GOBI, the leading acquisition platform for books and other academic content. EBSCO's NoveList service provides reading recommendations and enhanced content that can be integrated into library catalogs.

EBSCO has not been directly involved in the ILS business, though it is an important force in the discovery and electronic resource management arena. EBSCO Discovery Service competes with OCLC WorldCat Discovery Service and Ex Libris's Primo and Summon. Based on the EBSCOhost platform, EDS also extends access to the broader realm of scholarly materials beyond those covered in EBSCO subject database products. Reliable market share data is not available among the index-based discovery service products because the vendors report installations according to substantially different measures. We estimate, however, that EDS has far more installations than the other products in this category. EBSCO has worked with the vendors of over sixty ILS vendors to integrate EDS search results into their library catalogs or to enable EDS to serve as the catalog for the ILS.[2]

In addition to EDS, EBSCO offers products related to electronic resource management and access, including its FullText Finder and Holdings and Link Management based on the EBSCO Knowledge Base. EBSCO also distributes and supports the OpenAthens authentication service. In February 2019, the company acquired the Stacks web portal management platform for libraries. Its acquisition of Zepheira in February 2020 brought the foremost consultancy on linked data in the library arena into its fold. EBSCO has also made partnerships and investments in the area of open science, including with Code Ocean and Protocols.io.

EBSCO has entered the library services platform arena through its leadership and support for the open source FOLIO initiative. Along with other stakeholders, FOLIO aims to provide an alternative to Alma and WorldShare Management Services. Following a four-year development effort, the first library placed FOLIO into production in October 2019, with additional sites coming live in 2020.

FOLIO represents an important new competitive element in the academic library arena. In the future, academic libraries looking for new systems will include FOLIO in their considerations, expanding the viable options. Figure 2.2 shows EBSCO's development over time.

Follett

Follett School Solutions specializes in educational technologies in the PreK–12 school sector, with Destiny as its offering for school libraries and districts. A family-owned business with annual revenues exceeding $3.6 billion, the company operates a diversified array of business activities. It provides a major marketplace platform for schools to acquire educational content, it is a major supplier of textbooks, and it has many offerings in the broader educational content arena. Its Aspen student management system competes in the school district administrative applications sector.

In April 2016 Follett Corporation acquired Baker & Taylor, a major book distributor to libraries with a company valuation over $1 billion.

Compared to its other business activities, Follett's involvement in library technology represents a small portion of its revenue. That said, Follett School Solutions holds the largest market share in the US K–12 school library automation sector by far. Its Destiny ILS serves over 75,000 schools. Other than the libraries associated with international schools, almost all Destiny installations are in the United States. Although Follett created Destiny specifically for school libraries and districts, it also finds some use in small public and very small academic libraries.

Follett has been involved with ILS products for school libraries since the introduction of its Circulation Plus product in 1983. The company expanded in this sector through its 2006 acquisition of Sagebrush Technologies, which had previously acquired Winnebago Software Company and Nichols Advanced Technologies. Sagebrush had also created its own InfoCentre ILS for school libraries, which was released in 2005, but InfoCentre's development was discontinued shortly after Sagebrush's acquisition the following year. Figure 2.3 shows Follett's development over time.

OCLC

The nonprofit OCLC has a complex history of business acquisitions. Established in 1967 as a shared cataloging utility, the organization has expanded its service offerings into many different library-focused areas.

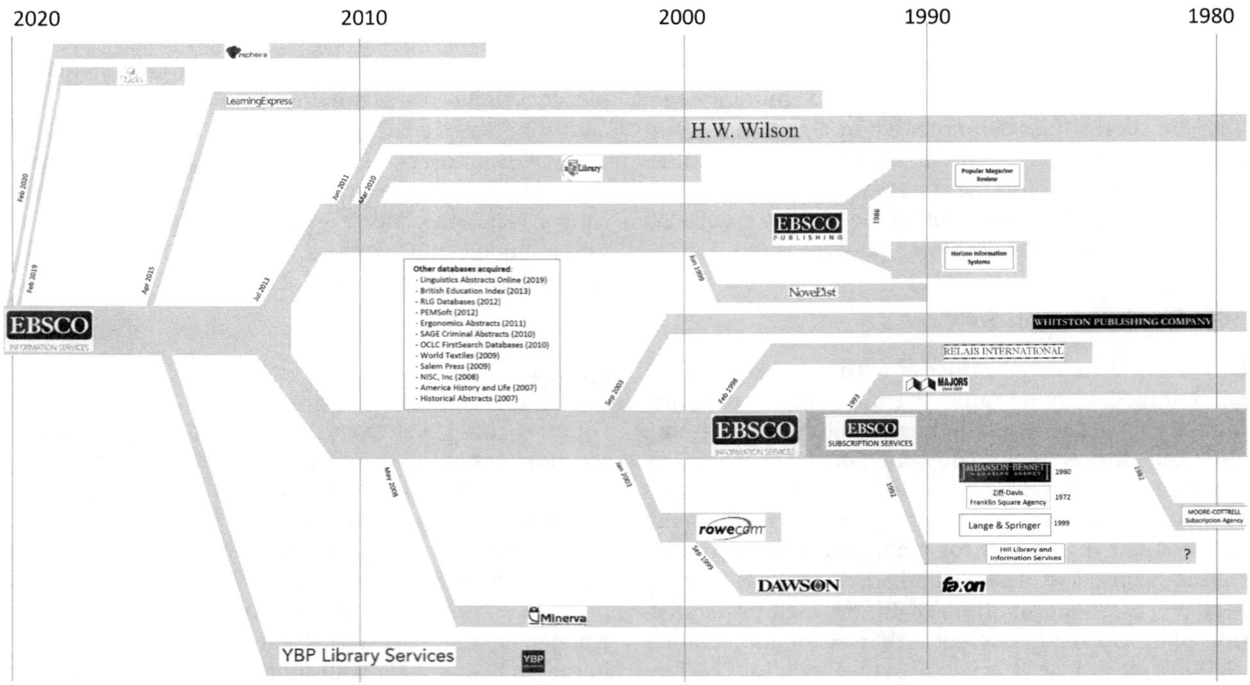

Figure 2.2
Development of EBSCO

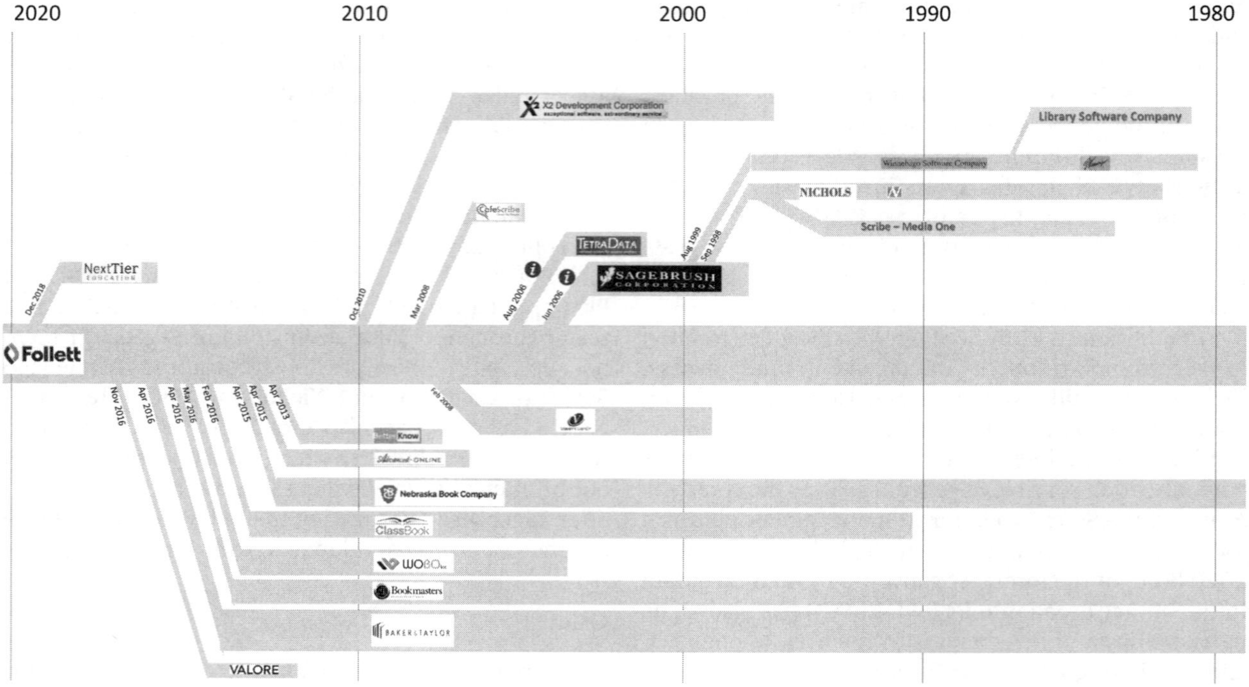

Figure 2.3
Development of Follett

With annual revenues of around $220 million, OCLC is a midsize organization relative to ProQuest, EBSCO Information Services, and Follett.

The acquisitions made by OCLC can be grouped into several threads. Several other nonprofit cooperative or service organizations have merged into OCLC, including WLN in 1999, CAPCON in 2003, 24/7 Reference in 2004, and Research Libraries Group in 2006. Some for-profit bibliographic services were acquired by OCLC, including Blackwell's B/NA Authority Service in 1997 and LTS Library Technical Services in 2000. It acquired the PICA cooperative based in the Netherlands and serving European libraries through a phased acquisition completed in 2007. PICA, now the basis of OCLC's EMEA operations, operates on a for-profit model because its services do not qualify as a charitable organization within European jurisdictions. While OCLC as a whole is organized as a US-based nonprofit, its structure also includes for-profit entities.

OCLC's involvement in the library technology industry is likewise complex and can be considered in three distinct phases. Beginning in about 1982, OCLC created a new Local Systems division within its organizations to market and develop library automation systems. OCLC acquired marketing rights to Total Library System from Claremont Colleges. It began a development project to create its own integrated library system named Local Library System (LLS). Development of LLS was discontinued in favor of enhancing a product named ILS initially developed jointly by the Lister Hill Center and Online Computer Systems, Inc. OCLC further enhanced the software, branded the product as LS 2000. OCLC marketed and supported LS 2000 beginning in 1983. Additional acquisitions made during this period included Data-Phase and its ALIS I and ALIS II systems. OCLC ended this chapter of involvement in the library systems arena in 1990 when it divested its Local Systems division to Ameritech Information Systems.

A second round of involvement began in 1993 with OCLC's acquisition of Information Dimensions and its BASISplus document management technology, as well as the TechLIB ILS from Battelle Memorial Institute. These products were primarily oriented to the corporate library sector. OCLC sold Information Dimensions to Gores Technology Group in 1997 as an interim arrangement until Information Dimensions was acquired by Open Text in 1998.

OCLC began its third and ongoing phase of activity in the library technology industry in about 2000. That year OCLC began a phased acquisition of PICA, which had developed the CBS automation system for large-scale consortial automation and bibliographic services and LBS as an integrated library system for individual libraries. Beginning in 2005 OCLC began acquiring other companies offering integrated library systems and related products, including in 2005 Sisis Informationssysteme and its Sunrise ILS used in Germany, Switzerland, and the Netherlands; Fretwell-Downing Informatics in 2005 with its OLIB ILS; Openly Informatics in 2006 for its linking technology and knowledge base; DiMeMa and the CONTENTdm image management system in 2006; EZproxy in 2008 from Useful Utilities; AMLIB from InfoVision Technologies , which is based in Australia, in 2008; BOND GmbH in 2011 with its BibliothecaPLUS ILS used mostly in Germany, Switzerland, and Austria; and Huijsmans en Kuijpers Automatisering (HKA) and its bicatWise ILS used by most public libraries in the Netherlands. In the resource-sharing sector, OCLC acquired Relais International and its D2D product in 2018. OCLC continues to support and perform needed development on each of these acquired products.

Another thread of activity by OCLC in the library technology sector comes through its own development efforts. Beginning in about 2009, OCLC began the development of a new library services platform aligned with its massive WorldCat bibliographic database; it was launched in 2011 as WorldShare Management Services.[3] Initially offered to all types of libraries, WMS has become one of the main competitors for academic and national libraries.

In 2018, OCLC began a major new effort to extend the bicatWise ILS acquired from HKA and position it as its strategic offering for public libraries in the United States and internationally, branded as OCLC Wise. With Wise's built-in patron engagement services, OCLC markets it as a new type of product of interest to public libraries beyond the traditional ILS model.

While maintaining a long list of legacy ILS products used primarily in Europe, OCLC is an important competitor in the library technology industry for new product selections. WorldShare Management Services has garnered a respectable market share of the academic library sector, and its Wise product is a new contender for US public libraries. Figure 2.4 shows OCLC's development over time.

SirsiDynix: Recovery from a Rough Business Transition

One of the prime directives related to mergers and acquisitions in the library technology industry has been to avoid abrupt disruptions of the strategic products currently in use. Events following the merger that formed SirsiDynix and its acquisition by Vista Equity Partners invoked a harsh product strategy that was not well received by its customer base, led to many customer defections, and damaged the reputation of the company. The events related to the acquisition of SirsiDynix serve as a case study that shows other vendors how not to achieve success in the library technology industry.

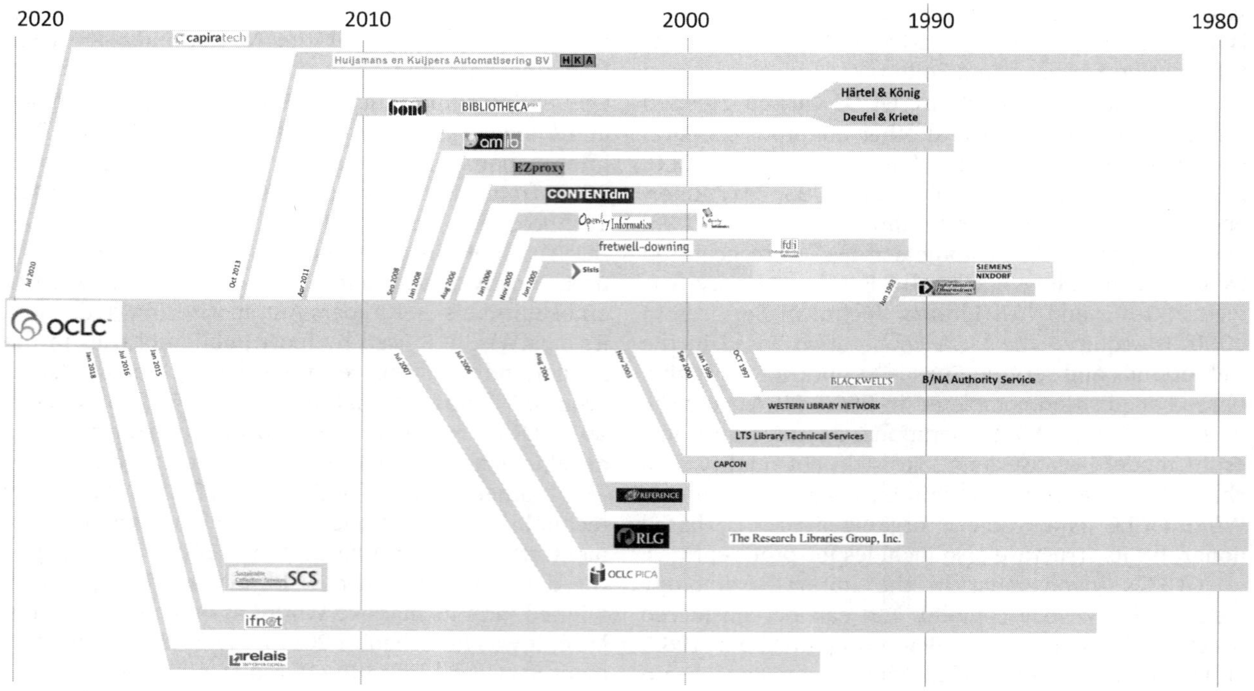

Figure 2.4
Development of OCLC

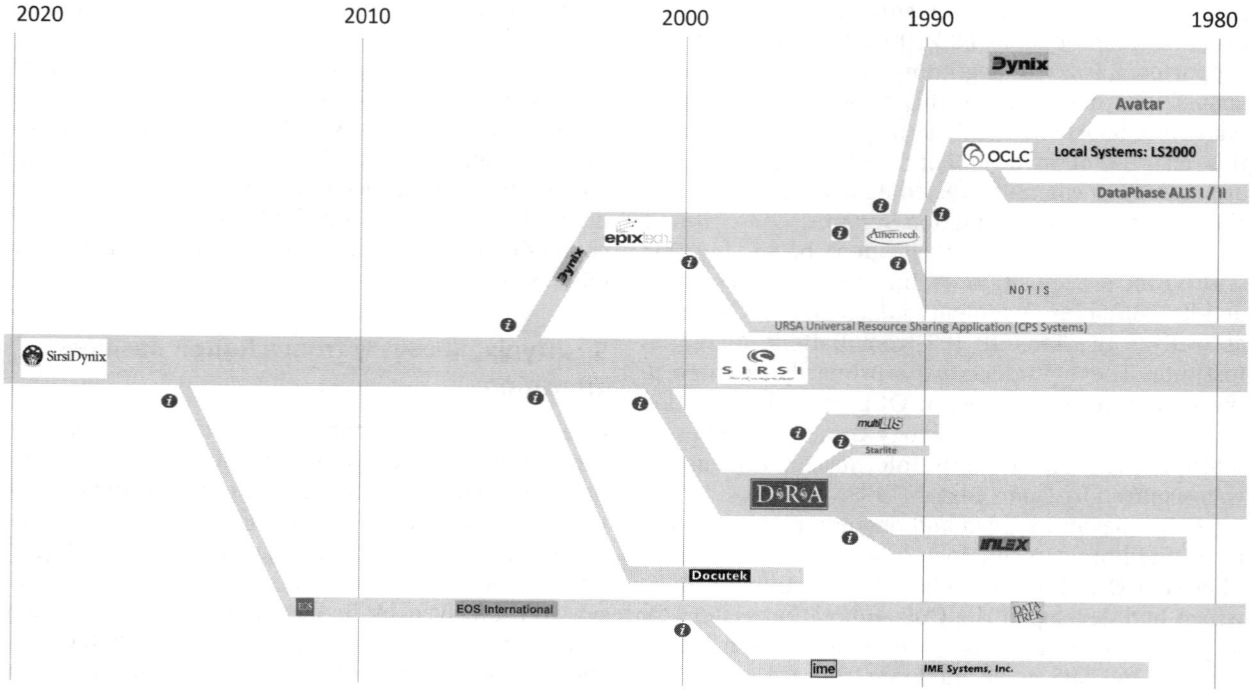

Figure 2.5
Development of SirsiDynix

Prior to 2005 Sirsi Corporation and Dynix were independent companies, each with its own product strategies. Each held a substantial market share in public and academic library sectors with some involvement in special and school libraries. The Unicorn ILS was the Sirsi Corporation's flagship product. Introduced in 1982, Unicorn was based on the Unix operating system and had a technical architecture based on APIs that proved to be a good foundation for long-term product development. By 2005 there were 1,512 libraries using Unicorn. Sirsi Corporation also continued to support for legacy ILS products DRA Classic, INLEX/3000, and MultiLIS, all of which were gained through its 2001 acquisition of Data Research Associates. Dynix supported three different ILS products. Its original Dynix Classic ILS, developed as a Pick application in 1983, had 768 installations in 2005. Horizon, the company's client/server product introduced in 1993, had 1,503 installations in 2005. At the time of the merger, Dynix Classic was a legacy product with diminishing installations; Horizon was in a phase of steady growth. Given the aging technologies of its ILS products and their slant toward public libraries, Dynix launched a new development initiative in 2002 to create a new system branded as Corinthian based on a modern technology stack and with functionality design that would also support academic libraries. Figure 2.5 shows SiriDynix's development over time.

With the backing of a group of venture capital firms, Sirsi Corporation acquired Dynix in 2005 and since that time has been known as SirsiDynix (DBA). The company was led by Sirsi Corporation's CEO Patrick Sommers. Following this transaction. Corinthian was positioned as the company's next-generation product. For libraries using Horizon, Corinthian would be offered as its next major version. Unicorn would continue to be developed, and libraries using Dynix Classic would receive support.

Vista Equity Partners acquired SirsiDynix from its founders and investors in December 2006. Following the abrupt resignation of CEO Patrick Sommers in February 2007, Vista principal Martin Taylor was given interim leadership of the company. Two months following the close of the acquisition, SirsiDynix announced a dramatic change in product strategy. Unicorn was positioned as the single flagship product for the company, initially temporarily renamed Rome and eventually rebranded as Symphony. Development of Corinthian was terminated. The current version of Horizon would continue to be supported but would not be further enhanced. Libraries using any of the legacy products—Dynix Classic, DRA Classic, MultiLIS, and INLEX/3000—were encouraged to migrate to Symphony. Any libraries that had intended to purchase Corinthian were offered Symphony instead. Although Symphony was positioned as a new product, it was entirely based on the Unicorn codebase, with the intention of including features planned for Corinthian as future enhancements. This product strategy was consistent with the playbook used by Vista Equity Partners for its portfolio companies to reduce costs through rapid product consolidation with a preference for mature products rather than those still in development.

This aggressive product strategy was not well received by the library community. Although some libraries took advantage of the enticements to move to Symphony, many others moved away from the company's products altogether. Figure 2.6 shows that, beginning in 2008, there was a surge of libraries moving away from Horizon. Only a few of these libraries opted for Symphony. Figure 2.7 shows only a small bump in the number of Symphony implementations in 2009. There were high numbers of defections away from Symphony at that time, which peaked in 2011 with 208 libraries moving to other products. The real beneficiaries of Vista's aggressive product strategy for SirsiDynix were Polaris, which saw a peak of 222 new sales in 2008, and open source ILS alternatives such as Koha and Evergreen. The open source ILS movement was invigorated by this event, driven by a heightened sense of distrust in vendors and hope that moving away from proprietary software would mean protection from future business events. Koha and Evergreen have seen steady growth in the US public and academic sectors since that time.

SirsiDynix was eventually able to mitigate the damage done by this unfortunate episode in its corporate history. In 2013 the company launched a product strategy emphasizing both Horizon and Symphony as flagship ILS products that would be enhanced and developed. At this time SirsiDynix launched its BLUEcloud initiative, which would create a new platform to offer web-based interfaces that would work with both Symphony and Horizon. The BLUEcloud platform would be developed incrementally until it addressed all staff functionality. This new product strategy has been well accepted by its customers and has helped reinvigorate sales for SirsiDynix.

Graphs reflecting SirsiDynix satisfaction scores from the Library Automation Perceptions Survey are available on Library Technology Guides: https://librarytechnology.org/perceptions/2019/#symphony

The International Library Automation Perceptions Survey provides a measure of how libraries have reacted to the company through this series of events. Libraries gave quite low satisfaction scores to the company in 2007, scores that dropped further in 2008. Scores have improved steadily since and are now relatively high compared to the other major companies represented in the survey.

The aggressive move toward a single-product strategy that SirsiDynix attempted has proven to be a lesson for the broader library technology industry. It has demonstrated to other companies and investors that abrupt changes in products or drastic cost-saving measures will not be well tolerated by libraries. All the mergers and acquisitions that have transpired in the industry since have given high priority to the continuity of products in use by library customers.

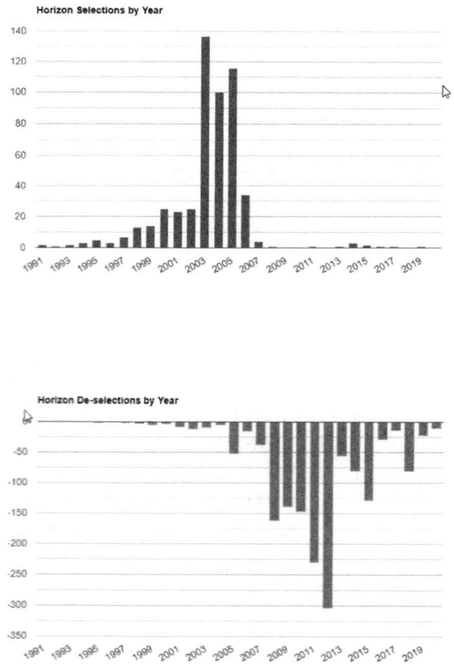

Figure 2.6
Horizon selections and deselections by year

> Sources for the path of Sirsi and Dynix include company press releases and my coverage in *Smart Libraries Newsletter* at the time of the merger:
>
> - Marshall Breeding, "The Chronicles of Dynix," *Smart Libraries Newsletter*, June 2005, https://librarytechnology.org/document/11896.
> - Dynix, "Dynix Announces Corinthian ILS for Academic Libraries," news release, April 8, 2005, https://librarytechnology.org/document/11386.
> - SirsiDynix, "Sirsi and Dynix Merge to Form SirsiDynix," news release, June 19, 2005, https://librarytechnology.org/document/11475.
> - Marshall Breeding, "SirsiDynix: The New Super-sized ILS Company," *Smart Libraries Newsletter*, August 2005, https://librarytechnology.org/document/11880.

The special library arena has a distinct set of requirements and is addressed by a set of companies different from those oriented to public and academic libraries. Special libraries have seen dramatic transformation, moving away from operating as traditional libraries with print collections to operating as information centers dealing primarily with electronic information. The consolidation in the corporate sector resulted in the elimination of many corporate and medical research libraries. The contraction in the special library sector translated into immense pressure on the companies reliant on sales to these institutions. Left in weakened positions, many of the companies specializing in special libraries consolidated into Lucidea. Previously known as SydneyPLUS, Lucidea has acquired most of its prior competitors, including Inmagic (2012), Cuadra Associates (2008), Eloquent Systems (2017), and Maxus (2018). Lucidea also acquired other companies offering document management and other technologies oriented to law firm libraries, including LookUp Precision (2010), Questor Systems (2010), LawPort (2007), and Insight Software (2003). Figure 2.8 shows Lucidea's development over time.

In the context of Lucidea's consolidated position, a few other companies remain in the competition. Soutron Global was established in 2012 by Tony

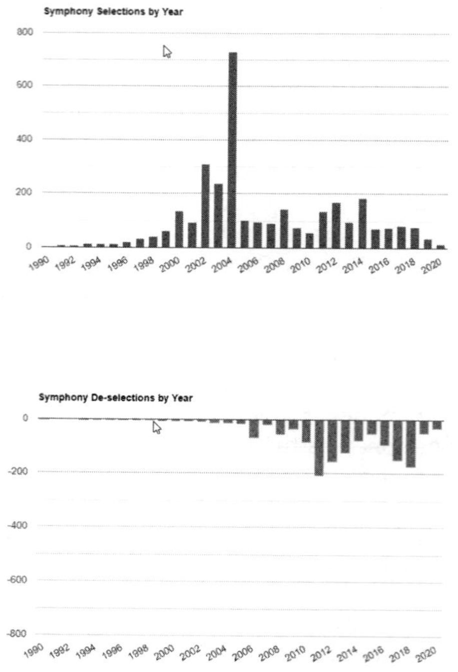

Figure 2.7
Symphony selections and deselections by year

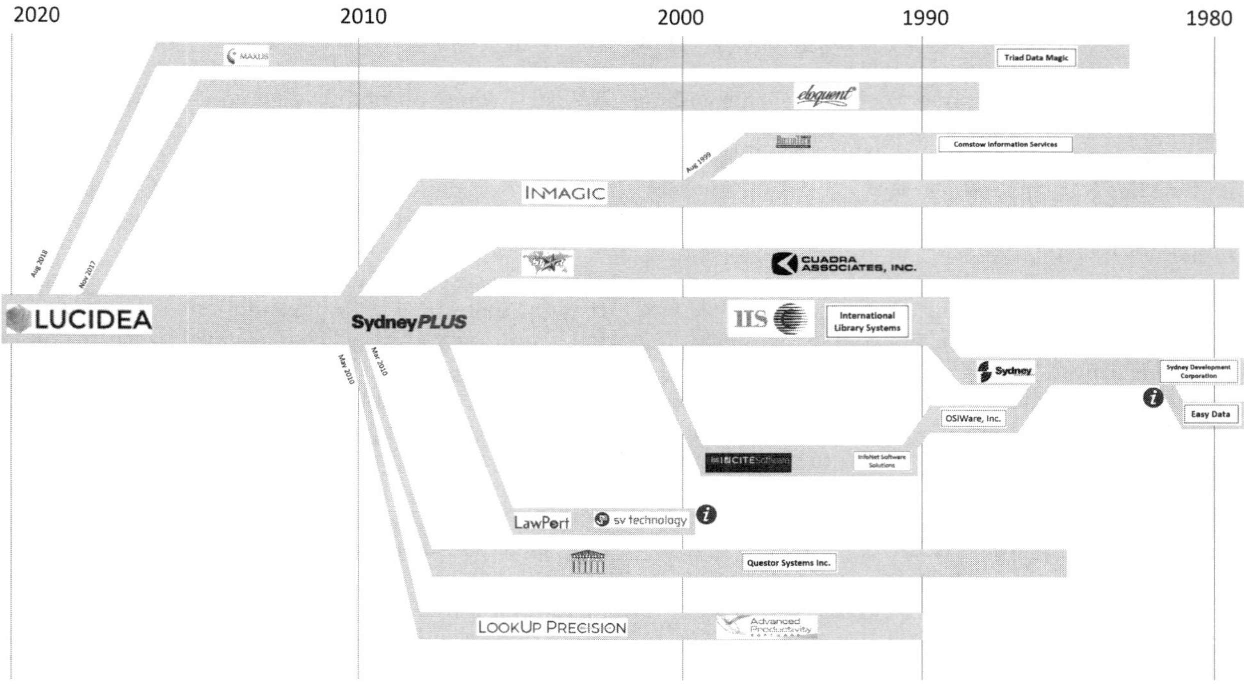

Figure 2.8
Development of Lucidea

Saadat in partnership with UK-based Soutron Limited. The EOS.Web ILS, created by EOS International, was acquired by SirsiDynix in November 2014. This web-based product was designed for special libraries and smaller academics.

The Library Corporation

A pioneering company in library automation, the Library Corporation has been creating and supporting library technology products and services since its founding in 1974. The company has remained under the management and ownership of its cofounder Annette Harwood Murphy. Over the course of its business history, TLC has offered a variety of products and services, mostly oriented to public and school libraries. Early products included MARC record databases and interfaces that continue today through its eBiblioFile service to provide catalog records for e-book collections and ITS.MARC as a general bibliographic and authority record service. TLC created the Library. Solution integrated library system for public libraries and school districts. It acquired the Carl ILS in 2000, which it has continually enhanced and redeveloped into its Carl.X and Carl.Connect product family designed primarily for large public libraries and consortia. The Library Corporation also acquired Tech Logic, a mid-level competitor in the library RFID and automated material handling sector, in 2005. The company has also launched a SmartTECH line of audiovisual products, computer peripherals, and products for library makerspaces and outreach programs.

The Library Corporation plays an interesting part in the history of the library technology industry. It has navigated through a succession of technology cycles and business trends, creating relevant products during each phase. TLC is currently the company with the longest run of founder ownership and management. The company has grown both through organic sales of its own products and relatively minor forays into business acquisitions.

Small and Midsize Competitors

Several companies continue to find good business opportunities at a smaller scale than the industry giants. They operate at lower levels of revenue, have limited capacity for development, but provide products and services valued by their library customers. Dozens of companies that operate mainly in the United States fall within this tier of the industry, and hundreds operate globally. Although even in aggregate these companies represent a relatively small portion of the total economic activity of the library technology industry, each fills a defined niche and contributes to the competitive dynamics.

Many smaller companies specialize in providing ILS products for smaller libraries. Their products are relatively inexpensive and appeal to libraries with limited budgets, including very small academics, small publics, and schools. Examples in this category companies include

- **Book Systems**, offering the web-based Atriuum ILS and its predecessor, Concourse.
- **COMPanion**, offering the Alexandria ILS used primarily in schools and small public libraries.
- **Biblionix**, offering the web-based Apollo ILS developed specifically for small to midsize public libraries.
- **Keystone Systems**, addressing the niche market of technology products for libraries serving persons with visual disabilities.
- **TIND**, a relatively new company established in 2015, that offers the TIND ILS, as well as institutional repository and resource data management applications. In the United States, TIND's products have been implemented by a handful of academic libraries, including academic law and medical libraries.
- **Media Flex**, which has developed the open source OPALS ILS used by schools and school districts. It has also been implemented in small public libraries, churches and synagogues, a few small academics, and a variety of organizations.

This tier of small companies plays an important role in the library technology industry. These organizations offer smaller or specialized libraries core technology products at affordable prices. The pricing of products from the larger players scale according to the size and complexity of a library but notoriously do not scale down to levels affordable by small libraries. These smaller companies can offer products with interfaces and functionality appropriate for libraries with less complex needs and boutique services. The large companies generally are not drawn to the modest revenues associated with serving smaller libraries.

Business Integration Following an Acquisition

Mergers or acquisitions result in some consistent patterns in personnel involved in the companies involved. The combined workforce inevitably contracts. The reduction of personnel costs is part of the business efficiencies expected in an acquisition. Business integration usually involves consolidation across all levels of the respective companies and is usually implemented over a lengthy time frame to ensure continuity of operations and services. Gentle, gradual transitions are especially important in the library industry, where abrupt changes could weaken the loyalty of customers and lead to defections to competing alternatives.

The first phase of integration generally happens at the executive level. A board of directors representing the interests of previous owners or investors will be disbanded. In cases where some residual ownership stakes remain, there may be representation on the board of the acquiring company. The top-level executive team of the acquired company will usually be phased out. In the case of an acquisition by a private equity firm or other investment group, the appointment of a chief financial officer usually takes place quickly to manage the finances of the acquired organization in alignment with the interests of the new owners. Strategic leaders may join the executive team of the acquiring organization or may be retained in a consulting capacity to facilitate business integration. In some cases, executives of the acquired company may end up leading the acquiring organization. One example is the appointment of Matti Shem Tov, who had led Ex Libris, as the president and CEO of ProQuest.

Another early move usually involves administrative personal and systems. Moving to common financial and human resource systems, as well as administering the combined company through a single set of administrative personnel, reduces costs and unifies the combined company into shared business processes and planning.

Marketing and sales forces also usually combine, but at a somewhat later phase. It takes some time to integrate new products into marketing strategies and to cross-train personnel. In many cases an acquired product gains a wider potential customer base through an established national or global sales force.

When companies combine, library customers of all products involved expect support and development to continue at levels at least as effective as before. Companies also see benefits as they continue development and support of acquired products because perceived diminishment of customer support levels can drive defections of customers and stalled development will hamper future sales. Companies usually blend business processes and customer relationship management as they work toward streamlined support channels. Development teams may also eventually combine to share tools or technical infrastructure.

Given the major savings in executive, administrative, and marketing functions, library technology companies can continue support and development of all incumbent products and still see substantial savings in operational costs. Only the most aggressive business strategies would target support or abruptly eliminate any incumbent products.

Opportunities for Product Innovation

The mergers of companies can provide an opportunity for creating new generation products. In some cases, all the products of the respective companies fall toward the end of their development cycle. This scenario presents multiple options for development strategy. The approach with lower costs focuses on expanding or modernizing one of the incumbent products. Though lower in risk and costs, such a strategy offers less long-term benefit. The viable life cycle of the product can be extended in the short term, but it can be extremely difficult to enhance a legacy product to meet long-term expectations that libraries will have for functionality and to reengineer its technology underpinnings to thrive in the modern information ecosystem.

The alternative strategy centers on development of a new product independent of the incumbent systems. New greenfield development avoids the complexities of modernizing obsolete technical components, including outdated programming languages, database technologies, or other frameworks not well suited for modern applications. This development strategy requires substantial investment but may also be less expensive than the work needed to modernize obsolete products.

The continuation of development of legacy systems not only benefits library customers, but also represents a profitable business model. Legacy products have mature functionality, require fewer new enhancements, and operate on stable technology. Any development needed to address security and interoperability issues or even to add new features incurs relatively low costs. The remnant customer installations, which in many cases are quite large, represent substantial revenue.

Maintaining and developing legacy products represents a very profitable business model in the short term. In the longer term, such a strategy fails to provide the company with products that may be viable in successive sales cycles. If the company's business plan focuses only on a short-term ownership cycle of five to seven years, which is typical for private equity investors, strategies based on extending the life of legacy products can be appealing. Corporate strategies concerned with long-term growth will create product road maps that extend decades into the future and that incorporate multiple rounds of investment in new products and technologies unconstrained by legacy systems.

The consolidation of the library technology industry wields two opposing dynamics. It narrows the choices available to libraries as they consider new products and technology providers. But consolidation also concentrates resources into a small set of organizations at levels able to create sophisticated products and services.

Product and Vendor Choices Narrow

Industry consolidation, through ongoing rounds of mergers and acquisitions, has narrowed the field of options available to libraries as they seek new technology products. Different dynamics apply to providers versus products. The concerns over uncomfortably narrow options among vendors are mitigated somewhat by the persistence of products. Many products have endured in the industry though multiple business acquisitions and often past the expected life span of their underlying technologies or the suitability of their functionality.

Library procurement processes assess not only the capabilities of each product under consideration, but also the capacity and reliability of its provider. The quality of support provided for a technology product plays a major role in evaluating potential products. Libraries also ask vendors to provide evidence that they are financially stable, have a positive track record of working with libraries of similar profile, and have the vision and capacity to enhance and evolve their products into the distant future. Since libraries tend to retain their strategic technology products for multiple decades, business disruptions or unexpected product transitions that transpire within these long periods represent major disturbances.

The number of vendors in the library technology industry has contracted steadily through mergers and acquisitions. The organizational charts (figures 2.1–2.5 and 2.8) document the absorption of dozens of antecedent companies into larger entities.

The contraction of products has followed a gentler trajectory. In almost all cases the products of a company continue to see similar levels of support and development following the acquisition of the associated vendor. The following section describes the business advantages of product continuity.

In the context of the tendency for product continuity through industry consolidation, several scenarios apply. Flagship products, aging legacy products, and development initiatives have seen different rates of survival through industry consolidation.

Flagship Products

Well-established strategic products with active pathways of product enhancements that remain in active sales cycles usually survive and prosper through business transitions. In recent times, examples include the following:

- **Symphony** and **Horizon:** Following an initial period of faltering, both incumbent flagship ILS products continue to be supported and developed. The BLUEcloud platform provided equivalent support for both. Only Symphony continues to see new sales. Horizon installations have declined.

- **Voyager:** Following its acquisition from Elsevier, Voyager has continued to see active enhancement and support by Ex Libris. Voyager, along with Ex Libris's own Aleph ILS, continues to see use by some of the world's largest libraries. Given the general neglect of Voyager under Elsevier, its life span was extended under the stewardship of Ex Libris.
- **Polaris:** Acquired by Innovative in 2014, Polaris continues to see active development and sales. Innovative has continued the advancement of LEAP, a set of web-based interfaces for Polaris. In recent months, Innovative has announced that Polaris will be marketed internationally, expanding beyond the bounds of the US and Canada, which previously had been its exclusive markets.[4]
- **bicatWise:** Acquired by OCLC from HKA in 2013, this product has become OCLC's strategic offering to public libraries. The product was already well established in the Netherlands, and OCLC began marketing WISE to public libraries in the United States, emphasizing its distinctive capabilities for patron engagement services.[5]
- **Carl.X:** Carl, a system designed for large public libraries and consortia, was acquired by the Library Corporation in 2005.[6] Since this acquisition, TLC has not only continued to support the product, but has substantially redeveloped its technical underpinnings, and Carl is the basis of TLC's Carl.X and Carl.Connect products, which it continues to sell to large public libraries.

Another formerly flagship ILS did not see much further attention following the acquisition of its associated company. Virtua, an integrated library system developed by VTLS, has not thrived since it was acquired by Innovative Interfaces. Although it continues to see active use in major public libraries such as the Queens Borough Public Library in New York City and in the Hong Kong Public Libraries, it has not been actively marketed by Innovative and its installations are rapidly declining.

In broad terms, we can observe that flagship products have strong survival rates following an acquisition. In most cases, it seems that these products endure as long as they would have under the antecedent vendor.

The survival of a product through a merger does not mean that the libraries using it will appreciate the change. In situations where the acquired vendor was not providing good support or was neglecting product development, the customer libraries may see the acquisition as a positive move. The perception can be more negative when the incumbent vendor was well regarded and the acquiring entity brings uncertainty. If a library selects product A over product B and the vendor for product B subsequently acquires product A, it may resent having to work with the vendor it specifically rejected. Through any of these scenarios, vendors must deliver positive performance to earn the trust of customers brought into their fold through a business acquisition.

Legacy Products Now Extinct

Legacy products may see an accelerated course toward extinction following a corporate acquisition. Independent of any business transitions, the number of installations of these products is declining and they are not actively sold. In the context of a business transition, the new owners may have less interest in the continuity of legacy products. The ongoing revenue and low support costs associated with legacy products make ongoing retention of the libraries using these products important and represent opportunities for migration to current product lines. Following a business transition, libraries using legacy products may be offered attractive incentives to accelerate their migrations to new products. Regardless of circumstances, some libraries continue to use ILS products well beyond official terms of support. For example:

- **NOTIS**, acquired by Ameritech in 1990. The demise of NOTIS was inevitable since it ran on IBM mainframe computers, which fell out of use as they were displaced by smaller servers with more computing capability and substantially less cost.
- **Dynix Classic**, acquired by Ameritech in 1992. Ameritech supported its ongoing maintenance but also developed the Horizon ILS based on current client/server architectures. Dynix operated on the once-popular Pick operating and database environment, which was displaced over time by the Unix operating system and relational databases.
- **Atlas (or DRA Classic),** the original ILS developed by Data Research Associates. DRA initiated the development of Taos to eventually succeed this legacy ILS that operated on the VAX/VMS operating environment, which was falling out of use.
- **MultiLIS,** originally developed by Sobeco Group and operated on VAX/VMS or Unix-based computers. It was widely implemented in libraries in French-speaking regions, including Quebec and France, though it eventually saw implementations throughout the United States. MultiLIS was acquired by Data Research Associates in 1994.

In the context of business consolidation, it is important to consider that these legacy products would have fallen out of use regardless. These products were unable to endure due to reliance on obsolete technical underpinnings, outdated functionality, or general lack of attention. Circumstances vary whether their demise would transpire more rapidly under a weakened independent company or within the portfolio of a larger consolidated entity. ILS products have a limited life expectancy. Industry consolidation may be only a partial factor in the demise of legacy products.

Development Initiatives

Products still in the development phase have not fared well through business transitions. The failures of these initiatives can be attributed to multiple factors. Some may be due to a simple lack of interest by the acquiring company in taking on an additional development initiative beyond the ones already underway within its organization. In other cases, the vision of the product or the technologies employed may have been deemed unworthy of ongoing investment.

Intota: ProQuest had begun an ambitious initiative to develop a new library services platform to compete with existing products such as Ex Libris Alma and OCLC WorldShare Management Services. This initiative proceeded in phases, with Intota Analytics as the first deliverable. The acquisition of Ex Libris essentially meant the demise of Intota. ProQuest ultimately chose to buy its way into the academic library technology sphere rather than complete its internal development agenda. Some libraries had implemented Intota Analytics, which continues to be supported by Ex Libris even though the full Intota library services platform was abandoned.

Corinthian: Dynix was well along in the development of Corinthian, also branded Horizon 8, at the time that the company was acquired by Sirsi Corporation. Although Corinthian was initially positioned as the strategic new generation platform for the combined company, the product was abruptly terminated once SirsiDynix was purchased by Vista Equity Partners. Corinthian showed considerable potential and was implemented in a small number of libraries. Its demise can be directly attributed to business decisions as part of a business acquisition. (See section SirsiDynix: Recovery from a Rough Business Transition for more details.)

Inspire: Innovative Interfaces had begun the development of a new generation platform branded as Inspire. This project was in the early development stage when Innovative was acquired by ProQuest. No libraries had placed Inspire Discovery or other modules of the product into production use. Initial messaging following the acquisition pointed to the withdrawal of Inspire in favor of a new technology platform to be created with the support of Ex Libris. The planned business integration of Innovative with Ex Libris and ProQuest has been paused pending the completion of a review of the acquisition by the FTC. In the coming months, the fate of Inspire or other development initiatives may be clarified.

For information on Inspire Discovery, see
Marshall Breeding, "Innovative Launches Inspire Discovery," *Smart Libraries Newsletter*, May 2019, https://librarytechnology.org/document/24466.

Taos: Stepping a bit further back into the history of the library technology industry, we can see Taos, a new product developed by Data Research Associates beginning in about 1995. Taos was intended to be the successor to its legacy DRA ILS and to the MultiLIS and INLEX/3000 products previously acquired. Taos was designed to follow the client/server architecture and to incorporate object relational database technologies. Although client/server products were considered progressive at the time, interest in object relational data stores was short-lived. The future of Taos came into question when Data Research Associates was acquired by Sirsi Corporation in 2001. Taos had been installed in production in several libraries but faltered in key sites such as the UCLA libraries. Despite initial messaging that Taos development would continue under Sirsi Corporation, by December 2001 a decision was announced that the company would focus its development solely on Unicorn because significant additional development would be needed to achieve even base ILS functionality. The demise of Taos came as a result of a combination of factors, including delays in development and unproven technology components, as well as pragmatic business decisions. Given many setbacks and challenges, it is difficult to assess whether Taos would have survived apart from the business decisions associated with the acquisition by Sirsi Corporation.

Source of Information on Taos
Sirs Corporation, "SIRSI and DRA Complete Merger: Integrated Company Announces Name, Organization, and Product Strategy," news release, December 11, 2001, https://librarytechnology.org/document/9434.

NOTIS Horizon: Horizon was a client/server development initiative initiated by NOTIS Systems in response to the increasing obsolescence of the mainframes on which its NOTIS library management system operated. This project was underway when NOTIS Systems was acquired by Ameritech. Dynix, also acquired by Ameritech, was developing its own client/server system known as Marquis. Shortly after the acquisition of both companies, Ameritech terminated the development of NOTIS Horizon and renamed Marquis to Horizon. This series of complex events was one of the earliest examples of a development initiative falling victim to a corporate acquisition.[7]

Competitive Dynamics

The ongoing rounds of mergers and acquisitions have made an impact on the options for core technology products for libraries in each sector. In the absence of business acquisitions, more products options may be available, but would there be more innovation? Without the formation of larger companies through consolidation, it seems less likely that there would have been the capacity to develop sophisticated products like the library services platforms that have seen wide adoption among academic libraries. The fragmented library technology environment yielded many different brands of integrated library systems but failed to develop new types of products to provide technology support in novel ways. During earlier periods, even the newer generation products that emerged were based on the model of functionality of the traditional ILS, though based on newer technical architectures and components (Taos, Virtua, Corinthian).

The competitive arena today, even in the context of a highly consolidated business environment, remains highly competitive, including products with meaningful distinctions. For academic libraries, current competitive options include the following:

- **Ex Libris Alma**, a library services platform based on proprietary software that has seen by far the highest commercial success. Alma emerged from a consolidated company, with major financial support from its investors. Aggressive development continues since its acquisition by ProQuest, including the creation of multiple follow-on products.
- **OCLC WorldShare Management Services**, which offers functionality and design similar to Alma's, though with meaningful differences relative to its inherent integration with the massive WorldCat bibliographic database. Although Alma and WMS fall within the same product category, they also embody substantial differences in functionality and vendor considerations.
- **FOLIO**, an open source library services platform initially launched with financial support from EBSCO Information Services and other stakeholders, such as the Open Library Environment and Index Data. Following a four-year development phase, FOLIO recently entered a cycle of production use by early adopters. Commercial support services for FOLIO are offered by EBSCO Information Services, Index Data, and ByWater Solutions in the United States as well as by many other vendors internationally.
- **Koha**, currently a viable alternative for academic libraries in the United States, especially with support arrangements from ByWater Solutions. In addition to adoption by large academic libraries such as Virginia Tech University, Koha with ByWater support continues to see inroads among midsize and smaller institutions.

Differing Trends by Library Type

The consolidation of the competitive environment in the library technology industry impacts each of its sectors differently. Each sector, generally defined by the types of library served, has followed distinct trends in the products adopted and in the business environment. These sectors overlapped more in previous phases of the industry. The overlap has diminished as each library sector diverged in terms of the characteristics of its collections and the types of services offered.

The products receiving active attention for new procurements carry the most weight when analyzing the competitive environment of each sector. It is especially important to consider the viable options available as libraries seek new systems and the relative selection rates.

The overall base of installed systems represents the outcome of previous competitive cycles. Some products that were successful previously may be legacy systems today. A product with a residual set of installations in a given sector but few new sales cannot necessarily be considered a top competitor for new selections. Products with decreasing numbers of installations and few new procurement selections should be considered legacy products and not strategic competitors. It is possible for a system to have the characteristics of a legacy product in one sector and of an active competitor in another.

Current Competition in the Academic Library Sector

Ex Libris Alma is currently the most successful product by far in the academic library sector. The product is on a progressive ten-year sales cycle where it has consistently won most new procurements. Alma was designed and developed specifically for academic and research libraries and offers very sophisticated functionality. Almost all libraries implementing Alma are affiliated with higher educational institutions or are national libraries.

OCLC WorldShare Management Services ranks as a secondary contender in the academic library sector. Although its volume of sales falls below Alma's, this product also has functionality well suited for academic libraries. Although it was originally offered to all types of libraries, in recent years sales have been made mostly to academic and national libraries. Many of the public libraries in the United States that originally adopted WMS have since moved to other products.

Sierra from Innovative continues to have a substantial installed base in academic libraries in the United States but makes few new sales in this sector. Some libraries remaining on Millennium ILS have upgraded to Sierra.

Koha, especially when supported by ByWater Solutions, has made substantial inroads into the US academic library market. In addition to a growing number of small and midsize academic libraries, ARL member Virginia Tech University has implemented Koha with hosting and support from ByWater Solutions.

The open source FOLIO library services platform has become the newest competitor among academic libraries. This product has recently moved beyond its initial development phase into early-stage implementations. Although the number of implementations remains small, it has generated strong interest and will be one of the main competitors going forward for academic libraries seeking to replace legacy ILS products.

Market Volume Analysis

The number of libraries selecting new systems has seen variation over the last two decades. Factors driving the number of libraries seeking new systems include the inability of the incumbent product to meet a library's operational requirements, the availability of systems perceived to offer improved support, and budget constraints. The total number of procurements made each year provides a basic measure, which can be placed into perspective by considering this number in proportion to the total number of libraries in the group.

The market volume among US public libraries can be calculated using data from Library Technology Guides and is shown in table 2.3. The line graph in figure 2.9 shows a rising sales volume between 2000, which reached its zenith in 2011. There was a sharp fall in new sales in 2007, which we attribute to the recession in that year, which negatively impacted library budgets. Since 2011 the number of procurement projects has declined steadily.

In the US public library sector, the turnover percentage—that is, the percent of libraries acquiring a new system relative to the total number of libraries—has ranged from a high of 8 percent in 2011 to a low of 2 percent in 2017. To smooth the trend lines, percentages have also been calculated as an average of adjacent years. This approach adjusts for large fluctuations due to variations in the timing of contract dates.

The volume of contracts per year among US academic libraries, shown in table 2.4, follows trends similar to those of US public libraries. There was more of a steady decline in contracts leading to the recession in 2008 followed by a rapid increase through 2011 (figure 2.10). The number of new contracts has declined since that year.

> We can anticipate that the COVID-19 pandemic crisis will have a strongly negatively impact on public library budgets. (See Panorama Project, "How Is COVID-19 Impacting Public Library Collections?" May 2020, https://www.panoramaproject.org/covid-19-impact-on-public-libraries; Public Library Association, "Public Libraries Respond to COVID-19: Survey of Response and Activities," May 2020, http://www.ala.org/pla/issues/covid-19/surveyoverview.)

The turnover percentage has been substantially higher in the US academic library sector compared to that of publics, ranging from a low of 14 percent in 2011 to a high of 31 percent in 2011.

The similarity in the trend lines of procurement volume for academic and public libraries can be attributed to the general economic environment that impacted both sectors. The recession of 2007–08 caused many libraries to defer the procurement of systems; in subsequent years, budgets became available to address pent-up needs.

The most striking difference in the procurement statistics between US public and academic libraries is the turnover percentages. A much higher proportion of academic libraries enter into procurement projects. This higher percentage can be attributed to the dynamic where they are not well served by their incumbent systems and replacement products are available with the potential to meet their requirements. The transition from legacy ILS products to new library services platforms, especially Alma and WorldShare Management Services, has been pervasive among US academic libraries. FOLIO likewise fits within this dynamic.

Among US public libraries, much of the activity has been lateral moves from one ILS to another with similar capabilities. So far, new products for public libraries with dramatically improved capabilities have not emerged. OCLC Wise and Axiell Quria have been positioned as transformational products but have not yet seen a significant market impact.

The declining number of opportunities in both the public and academic library sectors in the US is not good news for the vendors. The current pandemic crisis and associated economic decline will mean a further diminishment of new system procurements by

US public and academic libraries. A rapid economic recovery in combination with the availability of systems deemed able to deliver operational improvements could lead to an increase in opportunities, if the trends following the previous recession apply to the current scenario.

Updated graphs on number of contracts per year are available on Library Technology Guides: https://librarytechnology.org/products/procurements/

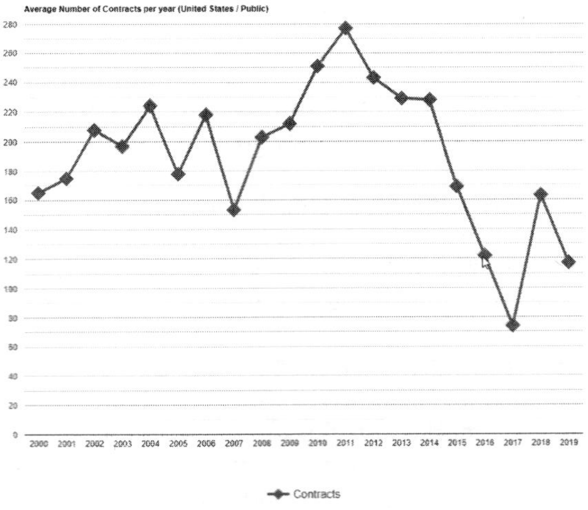

Figure 2.9
Number of procurements per year for US public libraries

Dominance versus Monopolies

Libraries would not likely tolerate an industry with only a single provider, whether for the entire market or for any given subsector. Nor would a monopoly be consistent with the regulatory framework in the United States. Innovation and pricing can suffer if the position of any single company stands unchecked through competitive forces.

Some companies in the library technology industry have gained a dominant position within their sector through business acquisition and organic growth. Follett's Destiny ILS has gained a market share of at least 70 percent among US public school libraries. Through it is more difficult to calculate its market share, Lucidea holds a strong position among special libraries, especially those in corporate or legal settings. ProQuest leads the academic and research library sector with its Alma library services platform and Aleph and Voyager ILS products. The recent acquisition of Innovative and its Sierra ILS extends that lead. No single vendor dominates among public libraries.

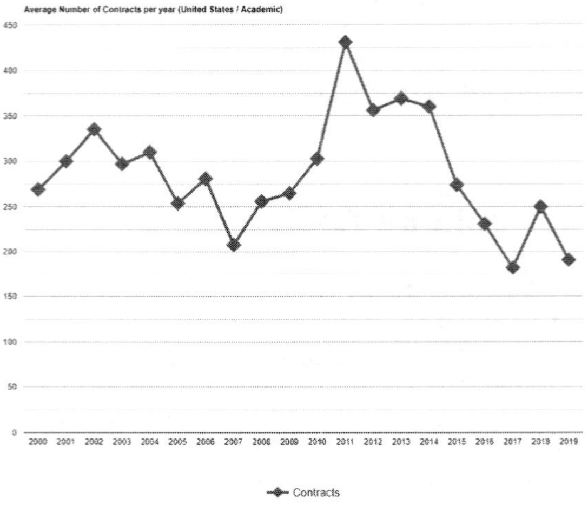

Figure 2.10
Number of procurements per year for US academic libraries

Table 2.3
Annual contracts for US public libraries

Year	2000	2001	2002	2003	2004	2005	2006	2007	2008	2009
Contracts	155	169	199	196	221	169	216	150	203	209
Turnover	4%	5%	5%	5%	6%	5%	6%	4%	6%	6%
Avg Contracts	162	174	188	205	195	202	178	189	187	220
Avg Turnover	4%	5%	5%	5%	6%	5%	6%	4%	6%	6%

Year	2010	2011	2012	2013	2014	2015	2016	2017	2018	2019
Contracts	249	276	233	228	219	168	118	72	161	116
Turnover	7%	8%	7%	6%	6%	5%	3%	2%	4%	3%
Avg Contracts	244	252	245	226	205	168	119	117	116	92
Avg Turnover	7%	8%	7%	6%	6%	5%	3%	2%	4%	3%

Table 2.4
Annual contracts for US academic libraries

Year	2000	2001	2002	2003	2004	2005	2006	2007	2008	2009
Contracts	253	285	303	283	299	231	267	197	248	254
Turnover	19%	21%	22%	21%	22%	17%	20%	14%	18%	19%
Avg Contracts	269	280	290	295	271	265	231	237	233	264
Avg Turnover	19%	21%	22%	21%	22%	17%	20%	14%	18%	19%

Year	2010	2011	2012	2013	2014	2015	2016	2017	2018	2019
Contracts	290	416	313	360	333	267	222	170	239	189
Turnover	21%	31%	23%	27%	25%	20%	16%	12%	17%	14%
Avg Contracts	320	339	363	335	320	274	219	210	204	142
Avg Turnover	21%	31%	23%	27%	25%	20%	16%	12%	17%	14%

Data on product installations does not reveal a monopoly in any of the library sectors. Selection tools in Library Technology Guides provide the means to assess the market share of products within library sectors. Though the completeness of the data varies, information on installations among US public and academic libraries is complete enough for detailed analysis. In the US academic library sector, Alma holds a 32.6 percent market share overall, though it is more dominant among specific subsectors, such as the members of the Association of Research Libraries (59.7 percent). When considering the market share for ProQuest across products, it holds a 50.4 percent market share overall, 83.9 percent among ARL members, 85 percent among libraries with large collections over one million volumes, and 47 percent for libraries with midsize collections (20,000 to 200,000 volumes). Among all US public libraries, market share is more equally divided, with 16 percent using Symphony, 12 percent on Polaris, 12 percent on Sierra, 5 percent using Library.Solution, 6 percent using Koha, and a long list of other products. Among the members of the Urban Library Council, 29 percent use Symphony, 27 percent Sierra, 21 percent Polaris, 7 percent Horizon, and 4 percent Carl.X.

For source of information on product installation market share, see
Marshall Breeding, "Marketshare Report," Library Technology Guides, https://librarytechnology.org/products/marketshare.pl.

Even among library types with a dominant vendor, significant competition remains. In the US academic sector, Alma sees competition from OCLC WorldShare, from Koha with support from ByWater Solutions, and from FOLIO. TLC's Library.Solution for Schools, Alexandria, Book Systems Atriuum, and OPALS give options in the K–12 school arena in addition to Follett's Destiny. The public library sector remains fragmented with no single dominant system or product. Internationally, local vendors in each country or region provide competition to the global players.

Notes

1. "About EBSCO: Leadership, Tim Collins" https://www.ebsco.com/about/leadership/tim-collins
2. Marshall Breeding, "Smart Libraries Q&A," *Smart Libraries Newsletter* (October 2017): 6.
3. See Marshall Breeding, "In Challenge to ILS Industry, OCLC Extends WorldCat Local to Launch New Library System," *Library Journal*, April 2009, https://librarytechnology.org/document/13927.
4. Marshall Breeding, "Innovative Interfaces Acquires Polaris Library Systems," *Smart Libraries Newsletter*, May 2014.
5. See Marshall Breeding, "OCLC Acquires the Dutch ILS Provider HKA," *Smart Libraries Newsletter*, November 2013; Marshall Breeding, "OCLC to Launch a New Product for US Public Libraries," *Smart Libraries Newsletter*, April 2018.
6. The Library Corporation, "TLC Purchases Tech Logic Corporation," news release, April 1, 2005, https://librarytechnology.org/pr/11367.
7. For more details, see Marshall Breeding, "The Sun Sets on Horizon," *Computers in Libraries*, 27, no. 6 (2007): 38–42.

Chapter 3

Industry Vendor Consolidation Study

This report documents the current state of consolidation in the library technology industry. Much of the revenue for core technology products is concentrated in few very large-scale organizations. The history of the industry is told in the rise and fall of companies and in the disposition of the products created. The life cycle of a product from launch, to general use in libraries, to a legacy status where new sales and installations decline, to eventual extinction is incredibly long. The emergence of a successful new product is a rare event.

In the context of ongoing industry consolidation, it is essential to be able to compare the competitive environment today to previous periods in the industry. Are fewer or more products available for libraries to choose from than in previous times? Are there fewer or more active vendors? To answer these questions regarding the competitiveness of the industry over time, an analysis was conducted using data from the libraries.org directory of libraries to measure the products implemented each year from 1990 through 2020 and the number of associated vendors. This study focused on academic libraries in the United States. The same methodology can be applied to other library sectors but would require the collection of additional data.

libraries.org
https://librarytechnology.org/libraries/

The key intent of the study lies in identifying the number of vendors and products active each year to be able to assess the relative levels of competition seen each year and to identify trends. These results and trends will provide important perspective on the degree of competition in today's heavily consolidated industry.

Methodology

The libraries.org directory has been developed as a data repository for the study and analysis of the technology products used by libraries. A variety of reports and visualizations have been developed that illustrate trends related to technology products currently used in libraries and general migration patterns. This study approaches the data somewhat differently to understand the technology trends as they have developed over the last three decades. Each libraries.org entry includes the automation system used by the library and those used previously (table 3.1). The data for the current and past automation systems has been collected since the inception of the database in 1997. While unevenly available for many sets of libraries, this data is most accurate for academic and public libraries in the United States.

The fields for automation systems are structured in libraries.org to portray the sequence of technology products used by each library, as shown in table 3.2. This study focuses on the fields related to tracking the integrated library systems or library services platforms and their respective implementation dates (ILS, InstallDate, PreviousILS, PrevInstallDate, PreviousILS2, PrevInstallDate2, PreviousILS3, PrevInstallDate3, PreviousILS4, PrevInstallDate4). While this structure can display the sequence of systems used, it is not conducive to supporting queries related to the systems used in a given year.

To support analysis related to the systems used in past years, the system sequence data needed to be converted into an annual chronology. The script that performed this analysis, shown in figure 3.1, dynamically created a secondary table that converted the sequences to annual data from 1980 to the current year for each of libraries targeted by the query.

This study addresses the dynamics between the automation products and the vendors responsible for them. Do the patterns of expansion and consolidation

Table 3.1
Original format for technology product sequences for a library

Technology Profile		
	Product Name	**Year Contracted**
Current Automation System	Alma	2017
Previous Automation System	Symphony	1996
Previous Automation System	NOTIS	1985
Previous Automation System	None	
Discovery Service (w/index)	Primo Central	2007
Discovery Interface	Primo	2007
Reading List Manager	Leganto	2017
OpenURL Link resolver	SFX	2004
Federated search product	MetaLib	
Electronic Resource Management	Verde	
Institutional Repository	DSpace	
Digital Asset Management	Locally Developed	
Item ID Type	Barcode	
RFID Provider	None	
Self-Check	3M SelfCheck System V-Series	
Automated Materials Handling	None	

The library's automation system is hosted by the vendor through an Software-as-a-Service (SaaS) arrangement.
This library is responsible for the procurement of the library automation system.

Table 3.2
Year-by-year product use for a library

Vanderbilt University Libraries	
2020	Alma
2019	Alma
2018	Alma
2017	Alma
2016	Symphony
2015	Symphony
2014	Symphony
2013	Symphony
2012	Symphony
2011	Symphony
2010	Symphony
2009	Symphony
2008	Symphony
2007	Symphony
2006	Symphony
2005	Symphony
2004	Symphony
2003	Symphony

Vanderbilt University Libraries	
2002	Symphony
2001	Symphony
2000	Symphony
1999	Symphony
1998	Symphony
1997	Symphony
1996	Symphony
1995	NOTIS
1994	NOTIS
1993	NOTIS
1992	NOTIS
1991	NOTIS
1990	NOTIS
1989	NOTIS
1988	NOTIS
1987	NOTIS
1986	NOTIS
1985	NOTIS

```
foreach my $LibraryID (@LibraryIDlist) {
        $SqlStatement="SELECT COUNT(*) AS librarycount FROM ilsdata WHERE
LibraryID = $LibraryID";
        &executeSQL($SqlStatement);
        $db->FetchRow();
        my $ExistingEntries = $db->Data("librarycount");

        if ($ExistingEntries > 0) {
                print "<p>There are already $ExistingEntries ilsdata records for
$LibraryID</p>\n" if ($debug eq "on");
                my $SqlStatement = "DELETE FROM ilsdata WHERE LibraryID =
$LibraryID";
                &executeSQL($SqlStatement);
        } else {
                print "<p>There are no ilsdata records for $LibraryID</p>\n" if ($debug
eq "on");
        }

        my $SqlStatement = "SELECT
Institution,ILS,InstallDate,PreviousILS,PrevInstallDate,PreviousILS2,PrevInstallDate2,Previous
ILS3,PrevInstallDate3,PreviousILS4,PrevInstallDate4 " .
          "FROM lwc " .
          "WHERE RecordNumber = $LibraryID";
        &executeSQL("$SqlStatement");
        $db->FetchRow();
        my (%data) = $db->DataHash();
        if (length($data{'ILS'}) > 0) {
                # proceed only if we have basic ILS data
    push(@MissingDates,$LibraryID) if ((length($data{'ILS'}) > 0)       &&
(length($data{'InstallDate'}) == 0)     && ($data{'ILS'} ne "None"));
    push(@MissingDates,$LibraryID) if ((length($data{'PreviousILS'}) > 0)  &&
(length($data{'PrevInstallDate'}) == 0)  && ($data{'PreviousILS'} ne "None"));
    push(@MissingDates,$LibraryID) if ((length($data{'PreviousILS2'}) > 0) &&
(length($data{'PrevInstallDate2'}) == 0) && ($data{'PreviousILS2'} ne "None"));
    push(@MissingDates,$LibraryID) if ((length($data{'PreviousILS3'}) > 0) &&
(length($data{'PrevInstallDate3'}) == 0) && ($data{'PreviousILS3'} ne "None"));
    push(@MissingDates,$LibraryID) if ((length($data{'PreviousILS4'}) > 0) &&
(length($data{'PrevInstallDate4'}) == 0) && ($data{'PreviousILS4'} ne "None"));
                my $CurrentField;
                my $ILS = "";
                my $FirstYear = 0;
                $FirstYear = $data{'InstallDate'}     if (length($data{'InstallDate'}) > 0);
                $FirstYear = $data{'PrevInstallDate'}  if (length($data{'PrevInstallDate'})
> 0);
                $FirstYear = $data{'PrevInstallDate2'} if
(length($data{'PrevInstallDate2'}) > 0);
                $FirstYear = $data{'PrevInstallDate3'} if
(length($data{'PrevInstallDate3'}) > 0);
                $FirstYear = $data{'PrevInstallDate4'} if
(length($data{'PrevInstallDate4'}) > 0);

                $FirstYear = 2010 if (($FirstYear == 0) && (length($data{'ILS'}) > 0));

                for (my $statyear=$fullyear; $statyear >= $FirstYear ; $statyear--) {
                        #Count down from current year through 1980
                        $data{'InstallDate'}     = 1980 if ($data{'ILS'}        eq "None");
                        $data{'PrevInstallDate'}  = 1980 if ($data{'PreviousILS'}  eq
"None");
                        $data{'PrevInstallDate2'} = 1980 if ($data{'PreviousILS2'} eq
"None");
                        $data{'PrevInstallDate3'} = 1980 if ($data{'PreviousILS3'} eq
"None");
                        $data{'PrevInstallDate4'} = 1980 if ($data{'PreviousILS4'} eq
"None");
                        $ILS = $data{'ILS'}        if (($statyear <= $fullyear)
&& ($statyear >= $data{'InstallDate'}));
                        $ILS = $data{'PreviousILS'}  if (($statyear <  $data{'InstallDate'})
&& ($statyear >= $data{'PrevInstallDate'}));
                        $ILS = $data{'PreviousILS2'} if (($statyear <
$data{'PrevInstallDate'})  && ($statyear >= $data{'PrevInstallDate2'}));
                        $ILS = $data{'PreviousILS3'} if (($statyear <
$data{'PrevInstallDate2'}) && ($statyear >= $data{'PrevInstallDate3'}));
                        $ILS = $data{'PreviousILS4'} if (($statyear <
$data{'PrevInstallDate3'}) && ($statyear >= $data{'PrevInstallDate4'}));

                        #Insert values into ilsdata tabel
                        if ($ILS ne "None") {
                                my $SqlStatement = "INSERT INTO ilsdata
(LibraryID,Year,ILS,DateCreated) VALUES ($LibraryID,$statyear,\'$ILS\',NULL)";
            print "<p>SQL: $SqlStatement</p>\n" if ($debug eq "on");
                                &executeSQL("$SqlStatement");
                                print "<p>$data{'Institution'} Year: $statyear $ILS</p>\n"
if ($debug eq "on");
                        }

                }
        } else {
     push(@MissingILSinfo,$LibraryID);
  }
    }
```

Figure 3.1
Segment for Perl script, which transforms system sequences to annual implementations

of the products differ from those related to the vendors involved? A year-by-year record of what vendor was associated with each system represents another factor in the analysis. This information was encoded in a two-dimensional hash that can be used to return the vendor associated with a product for any year between 1990 and the present.

Analysis of Academic Libraries in the United States

The libraries.org directory includes 3,016 academic libraries in the United States. This is the number of academic library organizations and does not count individual branches. These libraries vary from large research universities to smaller four-year colleges and include community colleges and small religious institutions. They do not include for-profit educational institutions, which often do not have formal libraries.

In 2020, fifty-nine ILS products are used among US academic libraries:

- Alma (956)
- Sierra (395)
- WorldShare Management Services (321)
- Symphony (314)
- Koha—ByWater Solutions (133)
- Koha—Equinox Software (7)
- Koha—LibLime (22)
- Koha—Nucsoft (1)
- Library.Solution (67)
- Voyager (62)
- Polaris (47)
- Millennium (44)
- Horizon (42)
- Destiny (40)
- EOS.Web (39)
- VERSO (35)
- Atriuum (31)
- LibraryWorld (27)
- OPALS (26)
- ALEPH 500 (22)
- Evergreen—Independent (18)
- Koha—Independent (11)
- Evergreen—Equinox Software (8)
- CyberTools for Libraries (7)
- FOLIO—EBSCO Information Services (6)
- FOLIO—Index Data (5)
- FOLIO—ByWater Solutions (3)

- TIND ILS (4)
- Insignia (4)
- Kuali OLE (1)
- Liberty (1)
- Evolve (1)
- Colleague (1)
- Virtua (5)
- Spydus (1)
- Winnebago Spectrum (2)
- Small Library Organizer Pro (1)
- EOS e-Library Service (1)
- SA3000 (1)
- GLAS (1)
- Infocentre (1)
- Accessit Library (1)
- OpenBiblio (3)
- TinyCat (1)
- campusSIS (2)
- Locally developed (2)
- ResourceMate (3)
- Surpass (1)
- Bibliovation (2)
- Circulation Plus (1)
- Mandarin M3 (1)
- Mandarin Oasis (12)
- Mandarin M5 (9)
- Populi (7)
- Athena (1)
- OasisSIS—Library Module (3)
- Alexandria (9)
- Librarika (2)
- Mandarin (1)

These products are supported by a total of thirty-six vendors:

- ProQuest (1,531)
- SirsiDynix (397)
- OCLC (321)
- ByWater Solutions (136)
- The Library Corporation (67)
- Follett (45)
- Independent (35)
- Auto-Graphics (35)
- Book Systems (31)
- LibraryWorld (27)
- Media Flex (26)
- PTFS (24)
- Equinox (15)
- COMPanion Corporation (9)
- CyberTools (7)
- Populi (7)
- EBSCO Information Services (6)
- TIND (4)
- Index Data (5)
- Insignia Software (4)
- Softlink International (1)
- InfoVision Software (1)
- Ellucian (1)
- Civica (1)
- PrimaSoft PC, Inc. (1)
- Space Amazing (1)
- Accessit Library (1)
- LibraryThing (1)
- Nucsoft (1)
- Equinox Software (7)
- Kanopy Apps Technologies (2)
- Jaywil Software Development (3)
- Surpass Software (1)
- Mandarin Library Automation (23)
- Oasis Technologies (3)
- Librarika (2)

See tables 3.3 –3.8 for lists of systems and vendors and how they've changed over the years.

In 1990 the library technology was more fragmented, with forty-three vendors offering a total of fifty-four products. No single vendor was dominant across the entire US academic library sector. The most popular product, NOTIS, still under the ownership of NOTIS Systems, Inc., had been implemented by about 20 percent of libraries in this sector. No other product held more than 10 percent market share. DRA (9.7 percent), PALS (9.4 percent), Dynix (8.8 percent), and Innopac were other popular products. The other products were implemented in smaller numbers. Figure 3.2 shows the trend lines since 1990 in vendors and products.

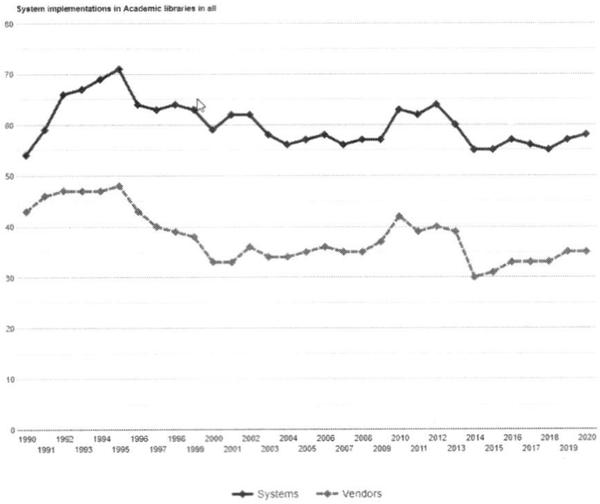

Figure 3.2
Product and vendor trends in US academic libraries: 1990–2020

Table 3.3
Products and vendors active in 2020

Year	Category	Count	Systems/Vendors
2020	Systems	58	TIND ILS (4); FOLIO—EBSCO Information Services (6); FOLIO—Index Data (5); Sierra (395); Symphony (314); ALEPH 500 (22); Insignia (4); Bibliovation (2); Evergreen—Equinox Software (8); Kuali OLE (1); Liberty (1); Horizon (42); LibraryWorld (27); Library.Solution (67); Atriuum (31); Evolve (1); Polaris (47); Koha—LibLime (22); Colleague (1); Virtua (5); Spydus (1); Winnebago Spectrum (2); Small Library Organizer Pro (1); EOS e-Library Service (1); SA3000 (1); Voyager (62); Infocentre (1); Accessit Library (1); VERSO (35); CyberTools for Libraries (7); Millennium (44); OpenBiblio (3); TinyCat (1); Koha—Nucsoft (1); FOLIO—ByWater Solutions (3); Koha—Equinox Software (7); WorldShare Management Services (321); campusSIS (2); Locally developed (2); ResourceMate (3); Evergreen—Independent (18); Surpass (1); Circulation Plus (1); Mandarin M3 (1); Mandarin Oasis (12); Mandarin M5 (9); Destiny (40); Alma (956); Populi (7); EOS.Web (40); Athena (1); OasisSIS—Library Module (3); Alexandria (9); Librarika (2); Koha—ByWater Solutions (133); OPALS (26); Mandarin (1); Koha—Independent (11)
2020	Vendors	35	TIND (4); EBSCO Information Services (6); Index Data (5); ProQuest (1,531); SirsiDynix (397); Insignia Software (4); PTFS (24); Equinox (15); Independent (35); Softlink International (1); LibraryWorld (27); The Library Corporation (67); Book Systems (31); InfoVision Software (1); Ellucian (1); Civica (1); Follett (45); PrimaSoft PC, Inc. (1); Space Amazing (1); Accessit Library (1); Auto-Graphics (35); CyberTools (7); LibraryThing (1); Nucsoft (1); ByWater Solutions (136); OCLC (321); Kanopy Apps Technologies (2); Jaywil Software Development (3); Surpass Software (1); Mandarin Library Automation (23); Populi (7); Oasis Technologies (3); COMPanion Corporation (9); Librarika (2); Media Flex (26)

Table 3.4
Products and vendors active in 2014

Year	Category	Count	Systems/Vendors
2014	Systems	55	WorldShare Management Services (211); Sierra (359); BiblioFile (1); Symphony (441); Horizon (73); Alexandria (10); Kuali OLE (2); Surpass (5); Alma (96); Millennium (327); ALEPH 500 (251); Evergreen—Equinox Software (14); Liberty (1); LibraryWorld (27); Voyager (401); Library.Solution (98); Insignia (1); Carl.X (2); Athena (3); Koha—PTFS (1); Koha—ByWater Solutions (57); Mandarin Oasis (14); Polaris (54); Virtua (7); Locally developed (2); Spydus (4); Koha—LibLime (26); Winnebago Spectrum (5); Small Library Organizer Pro (1); EOS e-Library Service (1); SA3000 (1); Destiny (43); Atriuum (19); OpenBiblio (2); VERSO (36); CyberTools for Libraries (8); Evergreen—Independent (19); Koha—Nucsoft (1); Circulation Plus (3); Infocentre (3); OPALS (15); Koha—Equinox Software (4); Koha—Independent (12); campusSIS (2); ResourceMate (4); Bibliovation (1); Mandarin M3 (3); Mandarin M5 (6); Librarika (1); Mandarin (2); Populi (5); EOS.Web (45); OasisSIS—Library Module (3); Evolve (1); Concourse (4)
2014	Vendors	30	OCLC (211); Innovative Interfaces, Inc. (747); The Library Corporation (101); SirsiDynix (560); COMPanion Corporation (10); Independent (37); Surpass Software (5); Ex Libris (748); Equinox (18); Softlink International (1); LibraryWorld (27); Insignia Software (1); Follett (57); PTFS (28); ByWater Solutions (57); Mandarin Library Automation (25); Civica (4); PrimaSoft PC, Inc. (1); Space Amazing (1); Book Systems (23); Auto-Graphics (36); CyberTools (8); Nucsoft (1); Media Flex (15); Kanopy Apps Technologies (2); Jaywil Software Development (4); Librarika (1); Populi (5); Oasis Technologies (3); InfoVision Software (1)

Observations for US Academic Libraries

The data from this analysis reflects some interesting trends and enables us to make interesting observations regarding the vendors and automation products during the last three decades. Figure 3.2 highlights the consistent pattern of the number of products active each year exceeding the number of vendors. Throughout the entire period, there were vendors supporting multiple products, gained either via previous acquisition or through new generation offerings.

This view of the data indicates that despite the consolidation of the industry, the number of competitors

Table 3.5
Products and vendors active in 2010

Year	Category	Count	Systems/Vendors
2010	Systems	63	Innopac (3); Millennium (764); BiblioFile (1); Symphony (493); Horizon (113); Voyager (503); Surpass (6); Evergreen—Equinox Software (6); Librarians Edge (1); LibraryWorld (19); Alexandria (7); Polaris (29); Library.Solution (98); Portfolio (1); Virtua (11); C2 (1); Dynix (12); Carl (2); GLAS (2); Atriuum (9); Mandarin M3 (6); Sierra (1); WorldShare Management Services (6); Koha—ByWater Solutions (10); Spydus (4); Koha—Equinox Software (2); ALEPH 500 (287); Small Library Organizer Pro (1); Winnebago Spectrum (14); ResourceMate (6); EOS e-Library Service (1); SA3000 (1); Liberty (1); Populi (1); Destiny (23); EOS.Web (32); Mandarin M5 (2); OpenBiblio (1); VERSO (28); OPALS (4); Advance (2); Evergreen—Independent (4); Koha—LibLime (38); Koha—Nucsoft (1); Circulation Plus (13); Mandarin (3); Athena (17); Unknown (1) No Vendor data for [Unknown]; Koha—Independent (7); LibrarySoft (1); campusSIS (1); Athenaeum (1); Locally developed (1); Bibliovation (1); Infocentre (16); Librarika (1); Mandarin Oasis (10); CyberTools for Libraries (8); Concourse (6); OasisSIS—Library Module (1); Readerware (1); BookCat (1); Evolve (1)
2010	Vendors	42	Innovative Interfaces, Inc. (768); The Library Corporation (101); SirsiDynix (618); Ex Libris (790); Surpass Software (6); Equinox (8); Hunter Systems (1); LibraryWorld (19); COMPanion Corporation (7); Polaris (29); BiblioMondo (1); VTLS (11); Contec Group (1); EOS International (35); Book Systems (15); Mandarin Library Automation (21); OCLC (6); ByWater Solutions (10); Civica (4); PrimaSoft PC, Inc. (1); Follett (83); Jaywil Software Development (6); Space Amazing (1); Softlink International (1); Populi (1); Independent (13); Auto-Graphics (28); Media Flex (4); Infor (2); LibLime (38); Nucsoft (1); New Generation Technologies (1); Kanopy Apps Technologies (1); SumWare Consulting (1); PTFS (1); Librarika (1); CyberTools (8); Oasis Technologies (1); Readerware Corporation (1); FNProgramvare (1); InfoVision Software (1)

Table 3.6
Products and vendors active in 2006

Year	Category	Count	Systems/Vendors
2006	Systems	58	Locally developed (5); Innopac (24); Millennium (697); BiblioFile (1); Symphony (464); Horizon (176); Voyager (527); Dynix (26); Surpass (5); Advance (5); Virtua (12); CyberTools for Libraries (6); Infocentre (18); Librarians Edge (1); PALS (6); Athena (26); DRA (9); Galaxy (6); Circulation Plus (19); Alexandria (7); Polaris (16); Library.Solution (96); C2 (2); Q Series (2); VTLS (1); GLAS (4); LibraryWorld (19); Mandarin M3 (6); Portfolio (3); Spydus (1); ALEPH 500 (281); Atriuum (2); Winnebago Spectrum (26); ResourceMate (4); EOS e-Library Service (1); SA3000 (1); Liberty (1); Populi (1); Destiny (18); Concourse (9); Koha—LibLime (1); Mandarin (4); Highland Library System (1); Mandarin M5 (1); OpenBiblio (1); Carl (9); MultiLIS (1); Koha—Independent (2); DB/TextWorks (1); Columbia Library System (1); Unknown (1) No Vendor data for [Unknown]; Amlib (1); LibrarySoft (1); Athenaeum (1); EOS.Web (18); Librarika (1); Mandarin Oasis (7); VERSO (6)
2006	Vendors	36	Independent (8); Innovative Interfaces, Inc. (721); The Library Corporation (106); SirsiDynix (675); Elsevier (527); Surpass Software (5); Infor (5); VTLS (13); CyberTools (6); Follett (107); Hunter Systems (1); Ameritech Library Systems (6); Polaris (22); COMPanion Corporation (7); Contec Group (2); EOS International (25); LibraryWorld (20); Mandarin Library Automation (18); BiblioMondo (3); Civica (1); Ex Libris (281); Book Systems (11); Jaywil Software Development (4); Space Amazing (1); Softlink International (1); Populi (1); LibLime (1); Highland Library System (1); Sirsi (1); Inmagic (1); OCLC (1); New Generation Technologies (1); SumWare Consulting (1); Librarika (1); Auto-Graphics (6)

active now is lower than some phases, but is not at its lowest point. The number of active vendors reached its lowest point in 2014 and has steadily increased since. Table 3.4 presents the products and vendors active in 2014.

Trends among the ARL Member Libraries

A data set of all academic libraries in the US represents a very broad group of libraries. Technology needs and favored products vary considerably for each tier of libraries organized by collection size, type of

Table 3.7
Products and vendors active in 2000

Year	Category	Count	Systems/Vendors
2000	Systems	59	Innopac (301); Symphony (282); Horizon (104); Carl (37); DRA (318); INLEX/3000 (6); Voyager (353); Dynix (155); Advance (22); NOTIS (95); ALEPH 500 (32); Locally developed (9); VTLS (22); Taos (4); KLAS (1); PALS (90); Athena (30); C2 (2); BiblioFile (5); Galaxy (25); Library.Solution (82); Millennium (220); Manager Series (1); Professional Series (1); PLUS (9); Circulation Plus (18); LibraryWorld (15); LS/2000 (1); Virtua (7); Portfolio (3); GLAS (5); CLSI (1); Polaris (6); LibraryCom (1); Librarians Edge (2); AARCS (1); OTHER (1); DataTrek (2); Infocentre (5); Amlib (1); Mandarin M3 (5); Winnebago Spectrum (32); Q Series (6); EOS.Web (13); Concourse (6); MultiLIS (44); Highland Library System (1); Mandarin M5 (1); DB/TextWorks (2); Columbia Library System (2); Mandarin (2); Unknown (1) No Vendor data for [Unknown]; Mandarin Oasis (5); Spydus (1); Destiny (3); GLIS (1); Alexandria (2); VERSO (1); CyberTools for Libraries (3)
2000	Vendors	33	Innovative Interfaces, Inc. (521); Sirsi (282); Ameritech Library Systems (194); The Library Corporation (124); Data Research Associates (372); Elsevier (353); epixtech (250); Geac Library Solutions (32); Ex Libris (32); Independent (9); VTLS (29); Keystone Systems (1); Sagebrush Corporation (67); Contec Group (2); Gaylord Information Systems (31); EOS International (28); Follett (21); LibraryWorld (18); OCLC (2); BiblioMondo (3); Geac Library Systems (1); Hunter Systems (2); NSC, Inc. (1); Unknown (1); Mandarin Library Automation (13); Book Systems (6); Highland Library System (1); Inmagic (2); Civica (1); COMPanion Corporation (2); Auto-Graphics (1); CyberTools (3)

Table 3.8
Products and vendors active in 1990

Year	Category	Count	Systems/Vendors
1990	Systems	54	Millennium (4); INNOVAQ (1); Ulisys (5); DataPhase (8); LIAS (1); Innopac (61); DOBIS (2); Symphony (20); NOTIS (211); Advance (23); LS/2000 (43); INLEX/3000 (19); LCS—Library Control System (8); PALS (101); DRA (104); Highland Library System (47); Voyager (1); Horizon (3); Dynix (94); MultiLIS (6); TOMUS (7); VTLS (46); OTHER (1); OCAT (1); BLISS (3); GLIS (51); Locally developed (22); PLUS (34); C2 (1); Galaxy (12); Manager Series (1); Professional Series (1); Q Series (2); BiblioFile (14); ALEPH 500 (2); Georgetown LIS (2); DataTrek (4); CLSI (28); GLAS (2); Micro-VTLS (1); UTLAS (4) (1); DB/TextWorks (1); Blue Star Library System (1); Gaylord System 100 Circulation (1); Mandarin M3 (1); Winnebago Spectrum (7); Circulation Plus (9); Columbia Library System (1); Inmagic (1); Unknown (1); LibraryWorld (1); VERSO (1); Carl (42)
1990	Vendors	43	Innovative Interfaces, Inc. (66); ULISYS Software Group (5); DataPhase (8); Penn State University (1); IBM (2); Sirsi (20); NOTIS Systems (211); Geac Library Solutions (108); OCLC (43); INLEX (19); Ohio State University (8); Unisys (101); Data Research Associates (104); Highland Library System (47); Carlyle Systems (8); Ameritech Library Systems (3); Dynix Systems (94); MultiLIS (6); VTLS (47); Unknown (1); OCAT (1); Biblio-Techniques (3); Independent (22); Contec Group (1); Gaylord Information Systems (13); Data Trek, Inc. (6); IME (2); The Library Corporation (14); Ex Libris (2); Georgetown University Medical Center (2); CLSI (28); EOS International (2); UTLAS Corp (4) (2); Inmagic (2); Ruf Corp (1); Mandarin Library Automation (1); Winnebago Software Company (7); Follett (9); McGraw-Hill School Systems (1); LibraryWorld (1); Auto-Graphics (1); Carl Corporation (42)

institution served, or other factors. Additional insight can be gained by looking at specific subsets. The members of the Association of Research Libraries constitute an important subset of academic libraries, representing those with the largest collections and most complex operations.

In 2020, among the 125 ARL members, thirteen different systems were in use or recently selected. Note that in the libraries.org database, new systems are recorded once the library has made a formal and binding selection, even if the system has not yet been placed into production. Table 3.9 presents the products currently in use.

Among this group, ProQuest holds an 84 percent market share, including the products within both Ex Libris (71.2 percent) and Innovative (13 percent).

Table 3.9
Vendors and products in ARL libraries, 2020

Product Distribution			
Company	**Product**	**Count**	**Percent**
Ex Libris	Alma	74	(59%)
Innovative Interfaces, Inc.	Sierra	15	(12%)
Ex Libris	Voyager	10	(8%)
SirsiDynix	Symphony	8	(6%)
OCLC	WorldShare Management Services	5	(4%)
Ex Libris	ALEPH 500	5	(4%)
SirsiDynix	Horizon	2	(2%)
EBSCO Information Services	FOLIO—EBSCO Information Services	1	(1%)
ByWater Solutions	Koha—ByWater Solutions	1	(1%)
Innovative Interfaces, Inc.	Millennium	1	(1%)
Kuali Foundation	Kuali OLE	1	(1%)
Innovative Interfaces, Inc.	Polaris	1	(1%)
Not Automated	None	1	(1%)

It is also helpful to look at the implementation trends of the ARL members over time. One view of this trend was compiled by constructing a retrospective tabulation of system implementation statistics published on Library Technology Guides from the Internet Archive. The data is shown in table 3.10. A graphic representation of the system implementation trends is available on Library Technology Guides: https://librarytechnology.org/libraries/arl/ils-marketshare-trends.pl.

Library Technology Guides implementation statistics
https://librarytechnology.org/libraries/arl/ils.pl

Internet Archive
https://archive.org

Another view of the market share trends among ARL member libraries was created with the system data in libraries.org, using the same process as for the full US academic library group (described above). This analysis reveals that the period with the fewest active systems and vendors was from 2008 through 2011 (figure 3.3). Table 3.11 presents the active products and vendors in 2008.

Study Results

Based on data describing the products implemented in academic libraries since 1990, this analysis suggests that the library technology industry is more competitive today than it has been in previous phases. More products are active today, and they represent a more diverse profile of technology and business arrangements than in some previous periods.

Among the ARL members, products active today include proprietary library services platforms (Alma and WorldShare Management Services), open source library services platforms (FOLIO, Kuali OLE), and proprietary integrated library systems (Symphony, Sierra, Millennium, Polaris), as well as open source integrated library systems (Koha). Vendors include a nonprofit (OCLC) and several for-profit companies (ProQuest, EBSCO Information Services, SirsiDynix, and ByWater Solutions). By comparison, in 2009 all six active products were proprietary integrated library systems (Aleph, Voyager, Innopac, Millennium, Horizon, and Symphony), and all the vendors were for-profit (Innovative, SirsiDynix, and Ex Libris).

While consolidation has skewed the total number of implementations toward a lower number of vendors, the overall field of products and vendors is more diverse in 2020 than it was in 2009. The results of this analysis differ from an intuitive impression that the library technology industry has become less competitive in recent years.

Table 3.10
ILS products used in ARL libraries, 2000–2020

ILS Products used by ARL Libraries																					
ILS	**2000**	**2001**	**2002**	**2003**	**2004**	**2005**	**2006**	**2007**	**2008**	**2009**	**2010**	**2011**	**2012**	**2013**	**2014**	**2015**	**2016**	**2017**	**2018**	**2019**	**2020**
Advance	2	1	1	2	1	1	1	1	1	1	1										
Aleph	6	9	17	20	20	21	21	22	22	23	24	26	25	22	19	18	13	12	9	8	5
Alma													5	8	17	21	31	35	57	67	73
Amicus	1	1	1	1	1	1	1	1	1	1	1	1									
Carl	1	1																			
DRA	12	12	4																		
FOLIO																					2
Horizon	10	10	9	7	7	7	7	7	7	6	4	4	3	3	2	2	2	2	2	2	2
Koha																					1
KualiOLE															1	1	1	1	1	1	1
LocallyDeveloped	2	2	2	2	2	2	1	1													
Millennium	33	34	34	35	36	37	38	38	39	39	40	40	27	25	21	20	16	12	5	2	2
MultiLIS	1	1	1																		
NOTIS	12	10	2	1	1																
Sierra													10	11	12	13	17	19	15	14	14
Symphony	13	13	17	19	18	18	18	18	18	18	20	19	18	18	17	17	16	15	13	11	8
Taos	1	1	1																		
VTLS	2	2	1	1	1																
Virtua					1	1	1														
Voyager	26	26	33	35	35	35	35	35	35	35	35	35	35	35	31	27	24	24	18	14	10
WorldShare															2	3	3	3	3	4	5
Ex Libris	6	9	17	20	20	21	21	57	57	58	59	61	65	65	67	66	68	71	84	89	88
Ex Libris MS	5%	7%	14%	16%	16%	17%	17%	46%	46%	47%	47%	49%	53%	53%	55%	54%	55%	58%	68%	72%	72%
Innovative	33	34	34	35	36	37	38	38	39	39	40	40	37	36	33	33	33	31	20	16	16
Innovative MS	27%	28%	28%	28%	29%	30%	31%	31%	32%	32%	32%	32%	30%	30%	27%	27%	27%	25%	16%	13%	13%
SirsiDynix	25	25	21	19	18	25	25	25	25	24	24	23	21	21	19	19	18	17	15	13	10
SirsiDynix MS	20%	20%	17%	15%	15%	20%	20%	20%	20%	20%	19%	18%	17%	17%	16%	16%	15%	14%	12%	11%	8%
OCLC															2	3	3	3	3	4	5
OCLC MS	0%	0%	0%	0%	0%	0%	0%	0%	0%	0%	0%	0%	0%	0%	2%	2%	2%	2%	2%	3%	4%
Totals	122	123	123	123	123	123	123	123	123	123	125	125	123	122	122	122	123	123	123	123	123

Table 3.11
Products and vendors active in ARL member libraries in 2008

Year	Category	Count	Systems/Vendors
2008	Systems	6	Innopac (1); Horizon (6); Symphony (19); Voyager (35); ALEPH 500 (24); Millennium (39)
2008	Vendors	3	Innovative Interfaces, Inc. (40); SirsiDynix (25); Ex Libris (59)

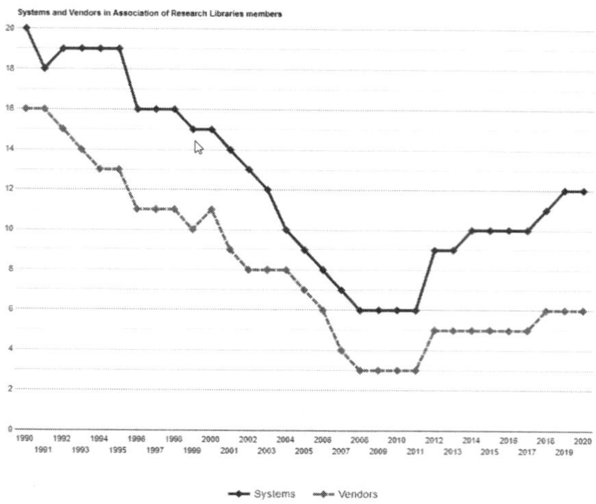

Figure 3.3
Products and vendors in ARL Libraries 1990–2020

Chapter 4

Concluding Observations and Resources

The previous chapters provide a descriptive account of the state of the library technology industry based on documented events and on trends revealed in historical data. This final section builds on these objective events and trends and offers some possible scenarios that may play out in the future. These forecasts must be taken with a large dose of skepticism. This discussion is meant to reinforce the reality that the industry remains in motion and that libraries must be vigilant regarding many possible outcomes.

Ongoing Movement among Current Players

EBSCO Information Services is a mature family-owned business that will endure indefinitely. The company has a pattern of regularly making new business acquisitions or partnerships. This trend will continue. Possible acquisition targets are varied. Will EBSCO eventually acquire an ILS vendor? It has previously avoided such a tack and now has embarked a strategy in the library services platform arena based on FOLIO and other open source initiatives. Recent partnerships reflect a growing interest in open science, opening the possibility of expanded business interests in the scholarly communications tools and analytics sector. Although EBSCO may continue to make some new acquisitions of content products, general activity in this area has slowed, with even Elsevier focusing on analytics and workflows for new business acquisitions.

ProQuest likewise will be a permanent fixture of the industry. Its current ownership status—including both family ownership and leveraged private equity investment—may change. The long-term maturity of the company may come through becoming a publicly traded company, though such a possibility is highly speculative. ProQuest will likely continue to make business acquisitions, though future possibilities hinge on the outcome of the FTC review of its acquisition of Innovative Interfaces. Should the FTC require any modification of that acquisition, it seems less likely that ProQuest would make additional investments in other ILS companies.

SirsiDynix will likely see a change in ownership in the next few years. While the length of investment periods varies among private equity firms, these ownership arrangements have limited duration. SirsiDynix has been owned by ICV since December 2014. This term of just over five years marks the typical time in which a private equity firm begins to consider its exit options. ICV Partners acquired SirsiDynix through its ICV III fund. Out of the eight portfolio companies involved with this fund, ICV has concluded only one investment to date. This suggests that ICV keeps its portfolio companies for a relatively lengthy term of investment and that it could retain SirsiDynix for a few more years. Companies acquired via this fund in 2013 remain in ICV's current portfolio. Possible arrangements when ICV exits this investment would include making follow-on investments or selling the company to interested investors or strategic acquirers.

The Library Corporation remains as the last founder-owned and -managed company in the industry. Although there has been no public messaging of an interest in selling the company, all the other longstanding founder-owned ILS companies have eventually sold to investors or strategic acquirers. VTLS, founded in 1974 by Vinod Chachra, was sold to Innovative in 2014; Innovative Interfaces, founded by Jerry Kline and Steve Silberstein in 1978, was sold to Huntsman Gay Global Capital and JMI Equity in 2013; Sirsi Corporation, founded by Jim Young, Jacky Young, and Mike Murdock in 1979, sold majority interest in the company to CEA Capital Partners in 1999.

General Product Trends

We are currently in a period where both legacy products

and new generation products are active. The legacy products will eventually wind down to extinction, representing a contraction in the number of active products. Specifically in the academic library sector, the number of libraries relying on Aleph, Voyager, Sierra, Horizon, and Symphony will decline as implementations of Alma, WorldShare Management Services, and FOLIO increase. Some of these traditional ILS products may endure longer based on the loyalty of libraries to the associated vendors. Trends for adoption rates of Koha in this sector are less clear.

We can likewise anticipate some contraction in systems among public libraries. The overall product distribution will narrow from the current fragmented state, though what systems might prevail in the longer term is less clear. Product trajectories among public libraries differ from those in the academic sphere. Beginning in about 2011, there was a widespread trend toward the adoption of library services platforms by academic libraries. The public library sphere lacks an obvious new product direction. Traditional ILS products continue to prevail. OCLC positions Wise as a new type of product, but it is early yet to predict whether it will gain widespread momentum. Axiell Quria has generated interest in Europe, though it lacks any momentum in the US even though Demco Software has signed on as its US distributor.

The two main open source integrated library systems, Koha and Evergreen, have seen consistent trends of moderate adoption that are not likely to be interrupted. A set of well-regarded companies provide support services enabling the use of these products by libraries without in-house technical expertise. FOLIO, the new open source library services platform, seems well positioned to become established as a competitor to the existing proprietary products. EBSCO Information Services, ByWater Solutions, and Index Data have each entered the fray of commercial support services for FOLIO.

The subsector of companies offering open source support services embodies many of the characteristics of the fragmented ILS sector in its earlier phase. Several companies are competing within a limited economy offering similar services. Given this challenging business environment, it would not be surprising to see formal or informal business partnerships in the future. The dynamics of this subsector differ from those in the proprietary software field due to well-established relationships of cooperative competition.

The Future of the Industry

There is little possibility that the path toward consolidation of the library technology industry has arrived at its destination. Space remains for future busines transactions. Changes in ownership arrangements of some of the companies are inevitable. We can expect at least some of these transactions to result in deeper industry consolidation.

The library technology sector faces a period of unprecedented challenges. The COVID-19 pandemic crisis has brought enormous disruption to libraries, and many will face devastating budget reductions in the short term from which they are not likely to recover quickly. Companies reliant on libraries for their ongoing revenues will face their own hardships. While revenue associated with existing contracts may be protected, it seems likely that the next round of sales of products and services will be bleak. Our market volume analysis reflected a downward trend for new system procurements already in place before the crisis. Further slowing of new sales opportunities will be exceptionally painful. This anticipated harsh business climate may accelerate the pace of future business transactions as weakened companies seek new, more sustainable outcomes.

Looking beyond current crisis conditions, the library technology industry seems likely to continue its movement toward a mature set of businesses, less dependent on temporary investment arrangements. We can expect some of the midsize companies under private equity investment or private ownership to become acquisitions targets of large-scale businesses within, or adjacent to, the library business environment. So far, the businesses making strategic acquisitions of library technology companies have been comfortably within the sphere of those already involved in related products and services. Future transactions may venture further afield. Businesses in the scholarly publishing sector come to mind. Given precedents such as Sage's acquisitions of Talis and Lean Library and the increasing involvement of Elsevier in workflow and analytics, it would not be unreasonable to suggest interest from this adjacent business sector. Another sector to watch for possible involvement in library technology companies might include educational technology businesses, especially those offering learning management systems.

Libraries can benefit when their technologies are produced by organizations able to set business strategies not bound by short-term financial goals. It is difficult to achieve substantial progress in product development when maximum profitability must be achieved within the midterm horizon of typical private equity investments. The multiple rounds of private equity ownership of Ex Libris, through which it produced multiple market-leading products, serve as the counterexample. But in very broad strokes, when small or midsize companies consolidate into enduring businesses such as EBSCO Information Services, ProQuest, Follett, OCLC, or Constellation Software, they can shift away from a constant mode of positioning themselves for eventual sale and work toward more sustainable long-term product trajectories.

Acquisition by one of these mature companies does not guarantee success. Personnel reductions, rigorous financial targets, and other aspects of business integration are the brutal reality of business acquisition. Yet the forced discipline of a new parent company, efficiencies offered by new technical and business infrastructure, and funding opportunities for development projects can help drive positive outcomes.

Consolidation has not turned out to be the death knell of the technology industry that many feared. The quantity of choices has indeed narrowed, but competition remains vigorous. Our analysis of the quantity of vendors and products active each year reveals more competition today than in past times. Especially in the academic library arena, meaningful differences can be seen among the systems options available today compared to the less differentiated products of the previous era. While future events cannot be predicted with certainty, we can reasonably expect further consolidation. Time will tell whether an ever more consolidated environment will yield strengthened technology systems or if it will constrain innovation.

Related Resources

This issue of *Library Technology Reports* draws heavily from the author's previous contributions to *Smart Libraries Newsletter,* also published by ALA. The list below also includes two articles that appeared in *Computers in Libraries.* Each of these articles documents key events as they happened. This report provides a broader perspective and demonstrates how these events have contributed to the broad evolution of the industry characterized by deep consolidation.

Breeding, Marshall. "Anticipating the Next Phase of the Library-Technology Industry." *Computers in Libraries* 36, no. 10 (December 2016): 16–18

———. "Axiell Acquires Bibliotekenes IT-senter." *Smart Libraries Newsletter* 39, no. 3 (March 2019): 3–5.

———. "Axiell Group Acquires Adlib Information Systems." *Smart Libraries Newsletter* 33, no. 4 (April 2013): 2-3.

———. "Consolidation Continues: Endeavor Acquired by Francisco Partners." *Smart Libraries Newsletter* 27, no. 1 (January 2007): 1.

———. "Consolidation Takes a New Form: BiblioCommons Acquired by Constellation Software." *Smart Libraries Newsletter* 40, no. 3 (March 2020): 2–5.

———. "EBSCO Acquires Stacks." *Smart Libraries Newsletter* 39, no. 3 (March 2019): 2–3.

———. "EBSCO Consolidates Its Library-Oriented Subsidiaries." *Smart Libraries Newsletter* 33, no. 7 (July 2013): 2–3.

———. "EBSCO Information Services Acquires Zepheira." *Smart Libraries Newsletter* 40, no. 4 (April 2020): 2–5.

———. "Ex Libris Acquires oMbeil, Introduces Leganto." *Smart Libraries Newsletter* 35, no. 6 (June 2015): 3–5.

———. "Ex Libris Acquires RapidILL." *Smart Libraries Newsletter* 39, no. 8 (August 2019): 2–5.

———. "Ex Libris Expands Learning and Research Division." *Smart Libraries Newsletter* 38, no. 9 (September 2018): 2–6.

———. "Ex Libris Group under New Ownership: Leeds Equity Sells Company to Golden Gate Capital." *Smart Libraries Newsletter* 33, no. 1 (January 2013): 3–5.

———. "FOLIO: Advancing from Vision to Software." *Smart Libraries Newsletter* 38, no. 1 (January 2018): 2–5.

———. "Follett Corporation Acquires Baker & Taylor." *Smart Libraries Newsletter* 36, no. 6 (June 2016): 3–6.

———. "FTC Reviews ProQuest Acquisition of Innovative Interfaces." *Smart Libraries Newsletter* 40, no. 5 (May 2020): 5.

———. "ICV Partners Acquires SirsiDynix." *Smart Libraries Newsletter* 35, no. 2 (February 2015): 2–6.

———. "Innovative Interfaces Acquires Polaris Library Systems." *Smart Libraries Newsletter* 34, no. 5 (May 2014): 3–6.

———. "Innovative Interfaces Acquires VTLS." *Smart Libraries Newsletter* 34, no. 7 (July 2014): 4–7.

———. "Innovative Interfaces Joins the Private Equity Club." *Smart Libraries Newsletter* 32, no. 4 (April 2010): 2–5.

———. "Innovative Launches Inspire Discovery." *Smart Libraries Newsletter* 39, no. 5 (May 2019): 3–5.

———. "Lucidea Acquires Eloquent Systems." *Smart Libraries Newsletter* 37, no. 11 (November 2017): 2–4.

———. "LYRASIS and DuraSpace Pursue Merger." *Smart Libraries Newsletter* 36, no. 3 (March 2016); 2–7.

———. "Lyrasis and DuraSpace to Merge." *Smart Libraries Newsletter* 39, no. 3 (March 2019): 5.

———. "Major Changes at Ex Libris." *Smart Libraries Newsletter* 28, no. 9 (September 2008): 4.

———. "Mergers of Non-profit Organizations Now Complete." *Smart Libraries Newsletter* 39, no. 9 (September 2019): 4–5.

———. "NFAIS to Merge into NISO." *Smart Libraries Newsletter* 39, no. 3 (March 2019): 6.

———. "OCLC Acquires German Public Library Vendor BOND, Extending Its European Presence." *Smart Libraries Newsletter* 31, no. 6 (June 2011): 2–6.

———. "OCLC Acquires the Dutch ILS Provider HKA." *Smart Libraries Newsletter* 33, no. 11 (November 2013): 2–6.

———. "OCLC Completes Its Acquisition of PICA." *Smart Libraries Newsletter* 27, no. 8 (August 2007): 1.

———. "OCLC PICA Acquires Fretwell-Downing Informatics Group." *Smart Libraries Newsletter* 25, no. 12 (December 2005): 1.

———. "OCLC to Launch a New Product for US Public Libraries." *Smart Libraries Newsletter* 38, no. 4 (April 2018): 2–4.

———. "OCLC's Ongoing Open Season on Acquisitions." *Smart Libraries Newsletter* 26, no. 2 (February 2006): 1.

———. "OverDrive to Change Ownership." *Smart Libraries Newsletter* 40, no. 2 (February 2020): 2–5.

———. "ProQuest Acquires Coutts from Ingram Content Group." *Smart Libraries Newsletter* 35, no. 6 (June 2015): 3–5.

———. "ProQuest Launches the Intota Foundation Release." *Smart Libraries Newsletter* 34, no. 8 (August 2014): 3–5.

———. "ProQuest to Acquire Ex Libris." *Smart Libraries Newsletter* 35, no. 11 (November 2015): 4–7.

———. "ProQuest Unifies Its Business, Drops Serials Solutions Brand." *Smart Libraries Newsletter* 34, no. 3 (March 2014): 2–6.

———. "SAGE Publishing Expands Its Tech Offerings." *Smart Libraries Newsletter* 38, no. 10 (October 2018): 3–6.

———. "SirsiDynix Acquires EOS International." *Smart Libraries Newsletter* 33, no. 12 (December 2013): 2–6.

———. "SirsiDynix ILS Set on Single Course." *Smart Libraries Newsletter* 27, no. 4 (April 2007): 1.

———. "SirsiDynix: The New Super-sized ILS Company." *Smart Libraries Newsletter* 25, no. 8 (August 2005): 1.

———. "Smarter Libraries through Technology: Consolidation and Concentration." *Smart Libraries Newsletter* 39, no. 3 (March 2019): 1–2.

———. "SOLINET, PALINET and NELINET Merge to Form Lyrasis." *Smart Libraries Newsletter* 29, no. 7 (July 2009): 2–3.

———. "The Sun Sets on Horizon." *Computers in Libraries* 27, no. 6 (June 2007): 38–42.

———. "SydneyPLUS Acquires Inmagic Assets: Continued Consolidation in the Special Library and Knowledge Management Solutions Arena." *Smart Libraries Newsletter* 31, no. 12 (December 2011): 2–6.

———. "SydneyPLUS Morphs into Lucidea Corporation." *Smart Libraries Newsletter* 33, no. 7 (July 2013): 5–6.

———. "Update on the Acquisition of Innovative by ProQuest." *Smart Libraries Newsletter* 40, no. 3 (March 2020): 2–5.

———. "Vista Equity Partners Acquires SirsiDynix." *Smart Libraries Newsletter* 27, no. 2 (February 2007): 1.

———. "WebFeat Acquired by ProQuest and Merged with Serials Solutions." *Smart Libraries Newsletter* 28, no. 4 (April 2008): 1–2.

Statement of Ownership, Management, and Circulation

Library Technology Reports, Publication No. 024-897, is published eight times a year by the American Library Association, 225 N Michigan Ave, Suite 1300, Chicago (Cook), Illinois 60601-7616. The editor is Patrick Hogan, American Library Association, 225 N Michigan Ave, Suite 1300, Chicago, IL 60601-7616. Annual subscription price, $340.00. Printed in U.S.A. with periodicals class postage paid at Chicago, Illinois, and at additional mailing offices. As a nonprofit organization authorized to mail at special rates (DMM Section 424.12 only), the purpose, function, and nonprofit status of this organization and the exempt status for federal income tax purposes have not changed during the preceding twelve months.

(Average figures denote the average number of copies printed each issue during the preceding twelve months; actual figures denote actual number of copies of single issue published neared to filing date: August/September 2020 issue.) Total number of copies printed: average, 556; actual, 526. Paid distribution outside the mails including sales through dealers and carriers, street vendors, counter sales, and other paid distribution outside the USPS: average 60; actual, 48. Total paid distribution: average, 321; actual, 288. Free or nominal rate copies mailed at other classes through the USPS (e.g., First-Class mail): average, 0; actual, 0. Free or nominal rate distribution outside the mail (carriers or other means): average, 9; actual, 7. Total free or nominal rate distribution: average, 9; actual, 7. Office use, leftover, unaccounted, spoiled after printing: average, 227; actual, 231. Total: average, 556; actual, 526. Percentage paid: average, 97.27%; actual, 97.63%.

Statement of Ownership, Management and Circulation (PS Form 3526, July 2014) filed with the United States Post Office Postmaster in Chicago, September 30, 2020.

Library Technology REPORTS

Upcoming Issues	
January 57:1	**Data Visualization with R for Digital Collections** by Monika Glowacka-Musial
February/ March 57:2	**Mobile Technology in Libraries** by David Lee King
April 57:3	**Video Accessibility** by Carli Spina